Motorcycle
Misadventures

**I'm sorry, but shouldn't there be
an apostrophe in that?**

Motorcycle Misadventures

hilarious short stories

Lived and Created by
Nathan L. Gibson

Illustrations by
Theresa McCracken

Design and Editing by
Kelsey Loftin

Also by the author

The System: Your Roadmap to Financial Independence

Motorcycle Safety

To reorder, visit www.motorcyclehumor.com or email Nathan directly at nathangibson900@hotmail.com.

ISBN: 978-1-5323-3313-2

First Edition: May 2013

10 9 8 7 6 5 4 3 2

On the cover: Jasper, my riding bud, in his favorite ride: Our 1976 BMW R90/6 with a Ural sidecar. Photo by Mary Amsler.

Dedication

Lenois Nathan Gibson
August 15, 1927 - September 25, 1990

Dad loved and was fascinated by all things mechanical. Fortunately, he loved to work on them too. He used to tell me that I could break an anvil. I am not sure what he meant by that though I suspect it was not intended as a compliment.

Before I was 14, he allowed me to buy my first scooter, an Allstate Fleetwood, made by Cushman and sold by Sears with a whopping 4.9 H.P. Briggs and Stratton motor! I saved my paper route and lawn mowing money and before you knew it I had the $294.50 to buy it.

There were four scooters/cycles to follow before I liquidated for my college fund. Dad could fix anything I could break and he kept them on the road. Perhaps he did this to keep me out of the house but whatever the motive, I appreciate it and the adventuresome 2-wheel part of my life that he inspired.

Misadventures

Acknowledgements

A number of my friends and family have encouraged me through the years to publish a collection of my documented escapades but none more persistently than Allan Arneil and Tony Baker. Thanks for your votes of confidence.

Kelsey Loftin had no clue as to my total disregard, even disdain, for spelling and grammar   conventions when she accepted the proofer assignment. The red ink flowed like the mighty Mississippi at flood stage, and the transformation happened. Her contribution went much further than proofing as she, also a writer, made helpful suggestions on clarification, arrangement and created the cover design. Visit www. dontpanicdm.com to learn more about her business, Don't Panic Digital Media.

A big thank you to a good friend, Larry Goldenthal, who read and reread the manuscript for suggestions on clarity.

The Sidelines Bar and Grill in Cedar Park, Texas, became our office around lunchtime each week for a few beers and a review of Motorcycle Misadventures. Thanks to Sidelines and our ever-smiling bartender, Sarah Pedro for cold beer and warm hospitality.

Theresa McCracken provided the customized "toons" and illustrations that introduce many of the stories. She read the blurb and coughed up whatever illustration it inspired. Thanks! Learn more about Theresa and her cartoons on www.mchumor.com. Other toons I share are not customized. However they hit my tickle bone and they fit. These are the work of Jerry King, Ralph Hagen and Scott Nickel.

For research, I was compelled to visit biker bars around the world to unearth carefully guarded secrets about what not to do on two wheels. "Hey, dude, what is the dumbest thing you ever did on two wheels?" In this regard, I give special commendation to ride buddies Phil Auldridge, Walt Conlin, and David Shiflet.

My research for the the safety tips you will find hidden in this book amounted to talking to bikers and motorcycle cops. There are too many contributors to single out but I must thank Sgt. Zumwalt who has made a career of training Austin motorcycle officers. His insight into moto safety is very impressive and much appreciated.

The love of my life, Susie Gallagher, contributed systems and marketing support as well as inspiration and encouragement.

Going Off Road

I have been a motorcycle guy for about as long as I can remember and can honestly say have never understood what folks get out of intentionally riding off-road. Every time I have gone off-road, I have collected scars on my body to prove that it was a bad idea. One of those scars I wear yet today is on the left side of my chest right above my heart.

It was not my fault. I was relaxing on a float in my backyard swimming pool having more than a few beers on a Saturday afternoon. I was pleasantly drifting in and out of sleep. All of the sudden, a four-wheeler came zipping down the hill of the vacant lot next to my house. After doing a few donuts on the flat part of the lot, he shot over the curb into the cul de sac and down the street. I did not like the sudden noise but what I really did not like is that I owned that vacant lot. Having spent the morning working on the landscaping the biker had just destroyed, I was not happy. Needless to say, I went from a period of relative bliss, bypassed anger and went into something akin to rage.

I owned two motorcycles at that time. One was a Harley and the other was one that could get me from point A to point B very quickly. My quick bike was a Honda Magnum V-65. As the street version of Honda's racing bike at the time, it had a 4 cylinder 118 H.P. engine that would take it's ultra-light frame to 100 mph in just a few seconds using only the first three gears. This left 3 more gears to wind before reaching a top speed of 165 mph. I loved that bike.

Without even drying off, much less thinking of putting on some jeans, I mounted that crotch rocket and was in hot pursuit of the aforementioned four-wheeler. I caught him less than a mile away, still in our neighborhood.

Upon pulling him over, he really pissed me off…with kindness. He apologized profusely and offered to come down and repair any damage done and in short was disgustingly nice.

Frustrated and with nowhere to dispense my anger and rage, I pointed the V-65 back toward home and gave it full throttle. The road was two lanes with one very sharp downhill curve. This combination set me up for a critical and even sobering decision to make. I was going into a 30 mph curve at about 70 mph. Do I lay the bike down with some hope of making the curve or do I nail the brakes slowing it down as much as possible before going "off-road"? Given that I was only wearing a flimsy swimsuit, laying that bike down and allowing the asphalt to eat all of my skin off did not seem appealing. I took door number 2. I nailed the breaks yet still hit the curb fast enough to launch the bike into the air. I held on and was still up right for about 25 yards before the bike went down. The bike stopped suddenly burying the handle bar into the dirt. I did not stop until quite some time thereafter. My flying body hit a number of small saplings but no large trees. I mostly just tumbled and slid in the dirt and gravel.

A very strange peace came about me when I realized that I was alive and could even get up on my own. I was not angry but almost happy, happy to be alive. I had a lot of blood on me from all the scraps and cuts. What I did not have on me was my swimming suit. I was totally naked in broad daylight in my own neighborhood. Most of my pain was coming from my chest where, by some weird circumstance, the clutch lever had broken off the bike and stuck into my chest. I should have left it there but like a fool I pulled it out. Blood spurted so I had to use one hand to apply pressure. After walking almost back to the bike, the rag that used to be my swimming suit appeared. With one hand over my chest as if I was pledging allegiance to the flag and the other holding my used-to-be swimming suit over my dick, I walked home past my neighbors who were doing Saturday afternoon things in their yards. They looked at me strangely.

Upon my arrival home, I banged on the front door. Jonathan, then about 12 years old, opened the door somewhat wide eyed. I told him to bring some towels and a fifth of Jack Daniels to the back yard. I would meet him there. I was far too bloody to go into the house.

I cleaned up pretty good, put some shorts on and went a few doors down where a friend's wife was a nurse. Fortunately, they were at home. She put a butterfly on the chest puncture wound and told me to get to the emergency room as soon as possible for x-rays and more attention to that puncture.

I would have done that except that I had a business event, a going away party for a friend, that very night and really needed to be there. I would catch the emergency room routine next time I go "off road".

As to the bike, I left it there for weeks just hoping someone would steal it. No one did but finally a guy came by and made me an offer as is, which I took and never saw that hot little number again.

On the road, imagine your ex has put a contract out on your head, and every automobile driver wants to kill you.

Assume these assassins are drunk. Assume they are texting. Assume they are stupid.

Watch your back.

"BUT OFFICER I AM ONLY ON THIS DANGEROUS ROAD HALF AS LONG IF I AM GOING TWICE AS FAST"

The Trooper With No Eyes

I met him toward the end of a great motorcycle trip. I had ridden with friends to Sturgis, at a time when 400,000-plus motorcycle enthusiasts descend upon a town of 6,770 South Dakotans.

One would think my faded Sturgis "Born to Ride" T-shirt would bring back memories of camping in the Black Hills or cruising up to the Mount Rushmore National Memorial or people-watching or enjoying the roadside hamburger joint with free beer and waitresses wearing only a smile and short shorts. One would think the night I drank too much and authorized the face of a large white wolf to be painted on my black leather jacket would be competitive. But the memory associated with that trip burned the most indelibly is my unplanned acquaintance with the trooper with no eyes.

Photo by Susie Gallagher

It turns out I had a beer or three the night before and authorized this airbrushed wolf on my new buffalo hide jacket. Wonder what I paid for it...

After four days of craziness in Sturgis, we rode across Wyoming and up to Red Lodge, Montana, for some riding in Yellowstone

National Park. Having "been there and done that," we broke up and went our separate ways. Some of the guys headed back to Ohio, one only had to ride to California. My goal was to get to Austin, which was just under 1,500 miles. I had only a day and a half before I was expected back at work.

Wyoming is beautiful on both ends with high-plains desert in the middle. Think the face of the moon decorated by a few random cactus and boulders. This is the bit we gave to American Indians in exchange for confiscating their lush Appalachian mountain lands of Tennessee and North Carolina. With nothing for the roads to go around, my pathway toward home was very straight and flat and boring. To solve this dilemma, I used my right hand on the throttle to turn up the excitement. The trooper with no eyes said I was going 97. I was trying to hold it to 100 mph. That was our closest point of agreement.

I had not seen a car much less another motorcycle for at least an hour. It should come as no surprise that the desert would be, well, deserted. He came out from behind a boulder and had to pull up beside me before I knew he existed. This small thing always gets my relationships with the arresting troopers off to a bad start. I cannot hear high-pitched sounds, especially sirens, over a Harley running almost wide open. I was not trying to get away from him. I was trying to get home.

"I been waiting for you all day," shouted an angry voice behind mirror-like reflective glasses wrapped around the sunburned face of a very big man wearing a star.

"Well, officer, I got here as fast as I could," I offered, trying to break the ice a bit.

One would think this would have had him rolling in the sand and laughing and giving me a warning ticket and advising me to have a safe trip home. Not. He just stared. I honestly did not know what to do. Should I hold my silence, too, or try to explain it to him?

He continued to just point those reflective glasses right down on me and not say a word. It was ire. I could not take it anymore, so suspecting he might have stopped me for breaking the speed limit, I blurted out. "Officer, the weather is perfect, the roads are straight, and other than you and me there is no traffic. Why would there be a speed limit on this road?"

The glasses finally broke silence only to say, "The animals."

Well, unlike my new friend, I do have an accomplished sense of humor, and for some unexplainable reason, I thought this was about the most ridiculous thing I had ever heard. Without thinking or dialing in my situation or considering my audience, I quipped, "Seems to me officer, you would allow the animals to go as fast as they please."

Holy shit! He did not get this one either. He stared silently again.

Finally, "Is there a good reason you were going 97 mph?"

"Yes sir, for safety reasons, sir. You must know that speed stabilizes a motorcycle. If I got off this motorcycle right now it would fall over. The faster it is going, the more stable it is. This is a matter of proven physics. But it is more than that. Half of all accidents are caused by rear-end collision. There have been no occurrences of vehicles traveling 100 mph getting hit in the rear, so you eliminate half the chance of having a serious accident. If that is not enough, all the accidents happen on the highway. By going twice as fast, you are on the highway only half as long, again cutting the chances of having an accident by 50 percent."

Seemingly unimpressed, he stared. At long last, he pulled a thick ticket book out of his pocket and proceeded to write me a citation for $187.50. As he handed it to me he finally made a complete sentence. "Now son, you're about to hit Colorado, and if you don't slow this thang down, they'll bust yo ass down there too."

He was wrong about Colorado. I did not get another ticket until I was almost to Dallas.

by Scott Nickel

If you have zero experience on two wheels, and your mid-life crisis has persuaded you to ride, please get a smaller, slower bike. Work your way up. Or... get the biggest, fastest, most badass ride you can afford. Just make me the beneficiary of your life insurance policy.

Bike Ride From Hell

T he 1,734-mile bike ride from Austin, Texas, to San Jose, California, took only two days and cost less than $300 for fuel, food, and one night's first class accommodation at the luxurious, roadside no-tell-mo-tel just west of Phoenix, Arizona. I rode 1,036 miles on day one without even getting a ticket. Now, I was stopped by a uniformed public servant just outside of Van Horn, Texas. I just told the officer that I had work in San Jose and had not found work in two years. I neglected to mention that I had not been looking.

He took one look at my loaded down '93 police bike and said "Don't you have a car?"

I replied truthfully, "Not one that will make this trip." The warning citation for speeding only took ten minutes. Day two was going to be a breeze, with only 654 miles to my destination.

In stark contrast to the start, the return trip took 11 days, and cost $6,213.37. You must be thinking that there is a story behind this and, yes, you are about to hear it. I am going to be kind and give it to you in brief summary points. The unabridged version of this sad tale would be longer than Gone With The Wind!

My Helmet's on Fire

Three hours into the trip, I smelled something burning. My brand new heavy weather Shoei helmet (which cost $300) was in flames. I had bungeed it to the saddle bag. It vibrated its way to and wedged between the back tire and the exhaust pipe. The helmet was ruined, and had worn a deep groove in the tire, making the tire unsafe for less adventuresome folks. The western side of California (Los Angeles area) has a Harley dealership about every 20 miles; the eastern side (desert) has a Harley dealership every 250 miles. I had little choice but to slow down to the speed limit and limp the 190 miles to the Bakersville Harley Davidson shop.

I Smell Gas

About 50 miles after the helmet incident, I smelled a strong gasoline odor coming from the right side of the bike. At about the same time, I saw something shiny and chrome bouncing down the road in my rearview mirror. After ten years of vibration, the bolt holding the air cleaner cover, which also protects the carburetor, had sheared off. I pulled over and saw that the uncovered carburetor was spilling gasoline onto my 800 degree Fahrenheit exhaust manifold. This created the potential of a fire at best, and an explosion at worst; neither of which is a good thing to happen between one's legs. So, with one totally unsafe tire and gasoline spilling all over my exhaust pipe, I crossed the interstate median so I could catch the nearest off-ramp to a (kind of) service station/inconvenience store.

A uniformed public servant came out from under a rock and provided me with instructional material about California laws regarding crossing a median. He was not amused when I pointed out that law enforcement officers do the same thing all the time. I did observe the officer step back to write the citation after he noticed the fuel spilling onto the manifold. Once he crawled back into his hole, I formed a makeshift air cleaner cover out of aluminum foil and eased down into Bakersville.

Bakersville Harley Davidson was predictably friendly, efficient, and expensive. While repairs were made to my bike, I had a beer or three with a new friend, Teddy, who was picking up his freshly serviced bike.

Only $437 and three hours later, I was happily on the road again, headed dead east into the Mojave Desert.

The Roach Hotel

For only $24.95, I stayed in the worst hotel I had ever seen, much less patronized. I have seen bigger cockroaches than the ones in this place, but not recently. The roaches didn't bother me much. Probably because I was preoccupied with the spiders and parking lot activity. I was up every 30 minutes or so, looking through the crack in the door to see if my Harley had been stolen. The mix of cars in the parking lot changed constantly through the night. Was I the only one there renting for an entire six hours? I made a mental note to splurge on a Days Inn next time, even if it did cost $44.95 for the stay.

My Third New Uniformed Friend

Unrested, but glad to leave, I was anxious for a change of luck, so I got off to a 6 a.m. start. I was not yet 100 miles down the road when I heard that familiar sound for the third time in three days. A uniformed public servant stopped me to see if I had read the latest on California speed limit laws. My instinct was to tell him that I had recently been serviced, but I passed on that.

My Private Desert Rest Stop

I fueled up just before entering the Mojave Desert. My plan was to pick up a couple of water bottles at this stop. However, the dilapidated

1968 Pontiac with a crooked rebel flag plate in the parking lot made me reconsider. It came complete with two rednecks drinking beer and smoking a joint. I was not going to leave my bike and gear in their care, so I filled up with my credit card and hit the desert.

At about the midway point between Blythe, California, and Phoenix, Arizona, I was driving on Interstate 10 through what seemed like a giant sandbox. That was when I encountered my next challenge. The temperature was 112 degrees Fahrenheit. The bike missed a few times; my imagination, I thought. I must be getting too hot and a little spooked at the thought of getting stuck out here. The engine missed again. Glancing over my shoulder, I saw billowing black and gray smoke coming from my exhaust. Then the engine blew with a horrific bang. The engine locked, putting me into a skid at about 85 mph. Next thing I knew, something broke loose, and the bike coasted to a halt. Oil was leaking from multiple locations on the engine block. This was not good.

This setback had the potential to give me some long overdue quiet time to commune with nature... and appreciate the sun's energy at *high noon... in the desert.* At high noon. In the desert. There was no sign of any shade, only cacti. I tried flagging down pickup trucks, but none would stop. I was far out of cell phone range. Traffic was sparse because sane people plan their desert travel at night or in the early morning.

A number of eighteen-wheelers passed by, but they were of little help. I was not going to leave my bike and my gear unattended and have it stolen. About the time I was beginning to rethink that strategy, someone appeared to be stopping.

It was the two rednecks in the 1968 Pontiac I had seen earlier. They both got out and meandered back. They were half drunk and smelled of beer and billy goat perfume. I had already pulled a spark plug out, mostly out of curiosity. I latched onto a hammer and a hunting knife, pretending to clean the plug. I told them I was down, but had gotten ahead of my ten Harley traveling partners. They would be picking me up any time now. The two asked me if I had any pot, then peacefully departed.

Periodically a biker would stop and give me a bottle of water, but most of the afternoon was spent waiting for a miracle. So I created a sun dial using a cactus and rocks. I guessed at what time it was, then checked my watch to calibrate the sun dial. Eventually, I got to within five minutes each hour. I also threw rocks at lizards and looked for snakes. Using a towel and three cactus plants, I fabricated a makeshift umbrella. Then I pulled up a rather large rock and began to make myself a bit of a camp. I even found a bottle half full of scotch in my bag and mixed it with the water donated by a passing biker. Life wasn't all that bad out there.

> Friends don't let friends drive on the interstate.

I had no ice for my scotch and water, but then most people who wake up and find themselves in hell probably don't have that luxury either. After about four hours, I broke down and trusted a biker with my credit card to send a tow truck from Phoenix out to get me. About five hours later, my tow arrived and things were looking up again. What a great adventure this had turned out to be! I was so happy, I didn't even try to negotiate the $325 tow charge with the driver.

The Runaway Wheel and Axle

The tow truck was a new Volvo, and the driver looked professional. He drove fast, which I liked. He did not bring iced-down beer, which would have been a nice touch. About 100 miles outside Phoenix, I witnessed my next once-in-a-lifetime potential disaster. The rundown pickup truck directly in front of us appeared to be moving sideways. At first, I wrote it off as the sun and the scotch, coupled with the heat and exhaustion.

Sure enough, the truck's axle had broken at the differential and was slowly coming out, with the wheel attached. The back of the truck started to wobble, and the axle and wheel separated from the truck, bouncing directly toward our snub-nosed Volvo tow truck. The left side of the pickup dropped to the pavement, riding on the wheel hub and immediately catching fire. Sparks were going everywhere, and the final resting place of the flaming truck was still to be determined. My tow truck driver handled it like it was just another day at the office. He headed for the median and dodged the bouncing wheel, never missing a beat. I just shook my head and said, more to myself than to the driver, "This has been an interesting trip."

My police special happily made it to the Harley shop. I walked up the street carrying a glove bag (roughly the size of a duffle bag that fits over the sissy bar on the bike), two saddle bags, and a stuffed tank bag. All that gear must have weighed 150 pounds. The bike probably blew the engine in protest! I dragged all that gear to the three hotels within walking distance before I could determine the best value. I ended up at a Residence Inn for $79 a night. After a shower and a couple of beers, I sat out by the pool to consider my options:

Option #1
Replace the engine with a new or rebuilt engine.

Option #2
Rent a U-Haul and take the bike to Austin, where I could work with a mechanic I trust.

Option #3

Sell the bike as salvage and take a flight home.

Option #4

Buy a new or used bike there in Phoenix.

Decision Time

My head told me to buy a BMW and start having less adventuresome travels. My heart would not let that 1993 bike go to the salvage yard after putting more than 150,000 miles on it. It had been rebuilt once before. I had driven it solo to Acapulco, taken it to England when I was assigned there, and driven it all over Europe.

In the end, I decided to have them put a new $5,000 motor in a $1,000 bike. Before I made my decision, the sales manager had one to make. He told the service manager that my bike had no trade-in value, and he did not want the bike. After I made the decision to buy a new motor, the sales manager humbled himself and approached me back at the shop.

He mentioned that I had not even looked at the new bikes he had on display. This provided the perfect opportunity for me to say, "If you don't want my bike, I don't want your bike either." I suspect that he took one look at my 16-year-old leather backpack and the age of my motorcycle, and he figured I wasn't a qualified buyer. You can't always judge a book by its cover.

Slow Is Painful on a Motorcycle

My instructions were to drive no more than 60 mph for the first 500 miles. That would put me in El Paso for the 500 mile oil change, after which I could drive normally. I thought I would never get to El Paso. I never realized how dangerous it is to drive 60 mph. When driving 90 to 100, you only have to pay attention to what's in front of you, because no one is going to hit you in the ass. At 60, you must look behind you as well.

From Phoenix to El Paso, I got passed by every truck and RV on the road. I had never been passed by a truck before! All I saw in my rearview mirrors all day long was very large chrome grills mere inches from my ass. Those grills were on trucks driven by pissed off truckers wondering why a motorcycle was slowing them down. After all I had been through on my journey, this was the most dangerous part. I must footnote that my gas mileage went up dramatically at this slow speed. This is interesting information, but certainly not useful, as it was not a speed I planned to leave on the menu.

Fur, Blood, and Guts Flew Everywhere

Barnett Harley Davison in El Paso is advertised as the world's largest Harley store. It showcases over 500 bikes and was certainly the largest toy store I have ever seen. They were very accommodating and had my oil and filter changed before I could finish a burger and beer at a nearby joint.

If you did not already think that I am a bubble off center, you will when you read that I actually left El Paso after already riding eleven hours. I thought I could ride all night and make it to Austin by morning. It did turn out to be a bad plan and no, I did not make it. In my defense, I was about to pee my pants to turn up the excitement on that new engine, especially after driving all day at 60 mph.

By 10:30 p.m., I was approaching Fort Stockton, Texas, bone tired and considering getting a room when a coyote made the decision for me. I got a good look at him right before I cut him in two. I was running 85 mph when he ran into the road. Had he kept up his speed, I might have missed him, but he stopped and glared right into the headlights. For a fraction of a second, he and I were both thinking, *"Oh shit!"*

Blood, shit, fur, and guts went everywhere. The sensation can only be described as hitting a large, spongy speed bump. I never swerved or braked. I just kept a death grip on the handlegrips and held her straight. The cycle went airborne for a second, but stayed straight. It went into a high speed wobble, but I never went down. I drove on for a while, deaf to my own thoughts and everything around me, before wondering whether the foul odor I smelled was coming from me or the coyote.

My feelings were a strange combination of fear, relief, and compassion for the coyote. I was wound tight by the sudden rush of adrenaline. I felt bad for the coyote. However, given the fact that I cut him in two pieces in under a nanosecond, I knew he was in coyote heaven before any part of him hit the road. Most of his guts, and more than a little fur, were on the front half of my new engine, my buffalo hide chaps, and my boots.

I decided to pull off at the first Fort Stockton exit and call it a day. I found a car wash at a truck stop and pressure washed most of the coyote off of me and my bike. I got a room at a Motel 6 and took a long, hot shower. I left my clothes outside hoping someone would steal them. I went to sleep feeling truly thankful that I did not drop that bike, having just spent over $5000 on the engine.

Safely Back at the Ranch

The balance of the trip was uneventful. I could have hired a limo from Austin to San Jose and gotten back for a lot less money. But then I wouldn't have a story to tell, would I?

Two Good Truckers, One Bad Spark Plug

Y ou cannot put more than a million miles on two wheels and not have a few close calls. This one was by far the closest I have come in my adult life to soiling my jeans.

I left Austin on my ten-year-old Harley FXRP one Friday around noon, finding myself about a hundred miles south of Little Rock, Arkansas, when it was time to call it a day. There are no really bad rides, but lower Arkansas is not much to write home about. The roads are pretty flat, and given that there is not much to go around, the roads are also straight. I was really looking forward to day two in the Ozark Mountains!

Traveling the back roads and headed as due North as I could manage, I got into view of the Ozarks about noon the next day. It was worth the wait.

It happened on Hwy 14 between Mountain View and Big Flat. The sun was bright, the air was clear, and the roads were beautifully crooked and mountainous. Perfect! Except that I soon caught up with an eighteen-wheeler who could barely get up the inclines on these mountain roads. Going down the curves also caused him to creep along, barely going the speed limit. Holy shit! I had ridden a day and a half to get to a motorcycle-worthy path. Now I'm staring at the ass end of a big, dirty, smelly truck going 55 mph. Disappointment and frustration were stressing me out. I could have pulled over and should have pulled over to give him thirty minutes, but I wanted to catch Branson, Missouri, in time for some live music that night.

For twenty miles that seemed like forever, I

was swerving into the oncoming lane every few minutes, hoping to catch a glimpse of a straight long enough for a safe pass. There were few oncoming cars, just oncoming blind curves and hills. The road was very narrow, barely wide enough for trucks to meet without slapping side mirrors.

Finally, there was a straight with only one minor problem: There was an oncoming truck in the distance. I had time to make a pass, so I dropped a gear and wound the Harley to about 3,500 rpm. When I got even with the driver's door of the truck, things were looking splendid. Then something dreadful happened: I lost power in one cylinder. In an effort to save my life, the truck I was passing began slowing down. He was trying to be helpful and let me pass, but with one cylinder down, I was losing speed too. We stayed neck and neck as the oncoming truck approached me head on.

I put the Harley exactly on the center line. Getting the idea, both truck drivers put one of their outer wheels off the road to give me as much room as they could. Neither one panicked, swerved, or hit the brakes; both maintained their cool and managed their rigs perfectly. My mirrors were just inches away from both trucks as the three of us flew by each other in formation, like Blue Angel stunt pilots, on that narrow road in the Ozark National Forest.

With the excitement over, the residual adrenaline had my heart throbbing like a jackhammer. I braked and pulled over to the nonexistent shoulder, allowing the bike to roll into a shallow ditch so I would be out of harm's way. I sat there straddling the bike for the longest time, somewhat numb, very relieved, and totally nauseated. Eventually, I began looking the bike over. I expected to see a lot of oil coming out of one of the heads, but there was none. After a little more investigating, I found that a spark plug wire had vibrated loose. It was dangling in midair, taking the bike down to 50 percent power.

I reconnected the plug wire, pushed the bike back on the road and fired up my baby. The one that had just tried to kill me. We eased on to Branson, silently thanking two damn good truck drivers and not so silently cursing my ten-year-old Harley Davidson.

According to studies by the Department of Transportation Safety Division, 38% of cycle fatalities involved riders who are over the legal limit. Now, I know you are a non-drinker and would never, ever have so much as one beer before mounting up. But do me a favor, and share this information with your hell raising friends!

What Am I?

I had done a 746-mile day on the BMW 1200RT, finding myself in Red Lodge, Montana, not surprisingly in a roadside biker bar. That first beer is always the best, and I was eagerly looking forward to it. With my leather jacket off and hanging off my seat, the helmet on the bar beside me, I waited with great anticipation as I watched the barmaid draft a 24-ounce Miller.

About that time a stunning young redhead sauntered up in tight blue jeans and plopped down right next to me. She immediately asked, "Are you a *real* motorcycle rider?"

"Well, I have had a ride now for over fifty years and have ridden all the states, including Hawaii and Alaska. I even took the Beamer up past the Arctic Circle. I have parcticipated in the Mad Sunday TT motorcycle race on the Isle of Man, near Ireland, twice. In 2003 I rode a fifteen-year-old Harley from Austin to Acapulco solo. I have ridden throughout Europe, Greece, El Salvador, Guatemala, Indonesia, and Australia. I rode sunup to sundown for two weeks on the South Island of New Zealand, covering every inch of paved road there and most of the gravel ones. I have challenged the Tail of the Dragon, the 11.5-mile trek with 318 curves on the Carolina-Tennessee Appalachian border. I don't know, I suppose some might say I am a REAL motorcycle rider. How about yourself?"

> A bike on the road is
> worth two in the shed.

She responded, "Well I go to bed thinking about naked women, I wake up thinking about naked women. When I shower I think of naked women. All I seem to think about is naked women. I think I am a lesbian."

Shortly thereafter she excused herself and left. Only a few beers later, a young man sat in what had been her seat. He asked, "Are you a *real* motorcycle rider?" I responded, "Well, I used to think I was, but I just learned that I am a lesbian!"

Your rear view mirrors are there for you to monitor, almost continuously, what is behind you. God gave you a neck to look over your shoulder before changing lanes. Don't rely solely on what your mirrors tell you. They don't always tell the whole story. Think of your mirrors as politicians!

I COULD SMELL THE TIRES BURNING,
THE MOOSE AND I THINK I MIGHT HAVE SMELLED MYSELF.

North To Alaska

A few years back, I found myself sitting in a bar on a Sunday afternoon where I overheard a guy talking about riding his motorcycle from Austin to the Arctic Circle. Well, after a few beers, that sounded pretty cool. Without hesitation or forethought (or any thought really), I decided to make that trip right then and there.

For one thing, it was a good reason to buy a new BMW 1200 LT for the trip. This bike is the most comfortable model and at 140+ mph, one of the fastest at that time. However, the 1200 GS would've been the smarter choice because the LT was much too heavy for the roads I would be riding. Then again, it was definitely cool: Push a button and the windshield goes up and down; push a button and the hydraulic kickstand drops down, picking you straight up; turn on heated seats, heated handle grips, plug-ins for heated boots and a vest—this bike even had reverse. The selling point that spoke to me was the exceptional range you could get with a 6 gallon tank and 40 mpg: Roughly 240 miles. I would be traveling up the Alcan Highway, starting at milepost 0 in Dawson Creek, British Columbia, and traveling northwest all the way to mile marker 1,365 in Delta Junction, Alaska. The Alcan was not known for frequent fuel opportunities.

Obviously, I cannot condense a 7,000-mile, one-month-on-the-road trip into a short story. I can however hit a few high points and a few low points. You'll just have to make the trip yourself to get the rest of the story.

The route was pretty simple. Starting from Austin, you try to head as north as you can while minimizing interstate travel. Enjoy the first 500 miles because that's how long you must ride to escape Texas. Now you only have

5 more states to traverse before hitting the city of Brandon, North Dakota, near the Canadian border. Roughly 1,100 miles later, you'll find yourself in Dawson Creek looking at post marker 0 of the famous Alcan Highway.

> Catching a yellow jacket in your shirt at 70 mph will double your vocabulary.

The highway was constructed as a strategic initiative on the part of the United States Military during World War II. It was built to move troops and munitions to Alaska in the event of an attack by either Japan or Russia. Troops had to hike over mountains and through valleys, cross many rivers, and cut through thick woods. The highway was completed in 1941 after about 9 months of construction by a group of 16,000 soldiers and civilians. The outsiders brought with them a lot of diseases, one of which being alcoholism, to the Indian tribes who had lived there contentedly for hundreds of years previous. In 1948, after the war, the Alcan Highway was opened to the public.

High Points

One of the high points of this trip include visiting Canada again. I've been a number of times but only to the larger cities in the east, and only to work on medical device projects. I had no clue how beautiful Canada is during its very short growing season. I was surrounded by orchards and wineries and vegetables of all types. Ditto for flowers. During this short growing season, the sunny days are long and the soil, having rested for 9 months, is very productive.

The wildlife sightings are abundant. Moose, elk, wild boars, caribou, foxes, wolves, and bears were not uncommon sightings (more on one specific moose when we get to the low points). A great thing about traveling the Alcan is that it's not a straight road, especially when it winds through the upper part of the Rocky Mountains. This made for perfect moto riding.

A major high point was a view of the snow covered Mt. Denali (20,300 feet) is absolutely breathtaking. Finally, after 4,000 miles on the road, I pulled into the roadside parking lot next to the Arctic Circle marker. Parking my bike next to two good friends made this trip even better—a major bucket list item checked right off!

Note: I must make a confession here because you're going to figure it out anyway: I cheated. After the ride up to the Circle, I split from the group in Fairbanks and headed to Anchorage. I had arranged to ship my bike to Seattle, Washington. I caught a train to a small town on the Intracoastal waterway. Waiting for me there was a 5 day luxury cruise down the Intracoastal to Vancouver where I knocked around for a couple of days. I then took a ferry to spend a few days in the beautiful city of Victoria. When it was time to go, Victoria was pleading with me to stay, but I managed to make it to the pontoon plane by takeoff. I was headed to Seattle where I would reunite with my bike for the 2,200 mile ride home.

My pontoon plane, or float plane, trip was a first for me. Landing on the water in Seattle was a trip. We flew right past the Seattle Needle on the way. I couldn't stay grounded. While on the cruise, I took a helicopter excursion from the ship to experience a glacier tour. The countless shades of blue and the overwhelming size of the glaciers were unlike anything I had ever seen.

Sometimes it takes a whole tank of fuel before you can think straight.

We landed on one of these ice cubes for a photo opportunity. The cruise happened to be a great time for snapping pictures. I love whales and it was the time of year for them to be feeding in the intercostal, so recorded lots of whale sightings.

I was not too impressed with Vancouver, but Victoria is one of the most attractive cities I have ever been to. It reminded me of Flores, France, with all its hanging baskets and charming streets. I went to a fish market there where they threw very large fish clear across the room to each other. These guys manage to catch these slippery fish with wet gloves on. How, I will never know.

Seattle gave me a chance to buy myself a cup of coffee at the very first Starbucks. After picking up my bike, I really enjoyed the ride across the lower part of Oregon. There was the perfect number of waterfalls and wineries along the way.

The last (and admittedly, best) high point of this trip goes to making a new friend who also spontaneously signed up for the ride to the Circle. David Shiflet and I share common ride habits, liking to get up early and get on the road. That way we would have time for side trips or make an early arrival. Neither of us like to ride in the dark, especially with 3,000 pound moose wandering around. As a side note, David was riding a Harley but after watching the performance of my BMW (from behind), he came home and bought all five 1200 models of BMW. "Why did you buy five new motorcycles, David?"

"Well," he said, "I didn't know which one I wanted!"

Low Points

To start down the list of low points from this trip: There were some very scary places on the Alcan. There had been a lot of rain on the highway, and parts of the road were caked in 5 or 6 inches of mud. We met logging trucks on crooked narrow roads—and they were not slowing down. My BMW, luggage, and myself weighed over 1,000 pounds and made me top heavy. Dropping a bike is bad enough, but dropping it in front or under one of those trucks gave me second thoughts about this adventure. Of course, looking back, it was a brilliant idea.

Most of the moose we sighted were at a pretty good distance, but a few were by the side of the road. They are much, much larger than a very large horse and are fairly quick on their feet but slow in their heads. They think nothing of charging a car, so a motorcycle certainly doesn't intimidate them. One ran out in the road in front of me and just stopped. I was running about 75 mph. The ABS brakes on that BMW saved my butt. I slid to within feet of an animal that I could have damn near slid under. I could smell the moose. I could smell my smoking tires. I could smell myself. After a pregnant pause, he sauntered on across the road.

That fancy hydraulic kickstand just about got me in trouble. I will admit that I was showing off, so maybe I deserved it. The Harley guys had carefully backed their rides into the gravel parking lot of our no-tell-mo-tel in Fairbanks. I whizzed in, not paying too much attention. I did not have to back in because my BMW had reverse. Still perched on the bike, with a big grin on my face, I hit the button for the kickstand to lift me up. It turns out, I had parked right over a pothole. One prong of the kick stand was hanging over it. One half had support, the other had nothing. The one that caught started pushed me quickly to the left. I caught the bike, but paid the price. I pulled a groin, working to hold it up until one of the guys came to my rescue. By this time, my smile had disappeared.

I kept pretty good notes on this trip, and I may decide to inflate this little story into a book one day. But please, do not wait for the book (or the movie). Regardless, you should experience this 7,000 mile adventure for yourself, so if you can take a month off and you like to ride, just go for this one. Looking back on it will forever put a smile on your face.

One last piece of advice before I let you go: Many of the towns on this route are over 100 miles apart, and many of them are one-hotel towns (if that). Unless you like sleeping with the bears, I suggest you book your motels well in advance.

> Never brake *and* swerve. To avoid an obstacle, you will have to make a quick decision. Hold her straight, and lock her down. Hit the front and back brakes, OR leave the brakes untouched and swerve. If you do both simultaneously, your ass is going down on the low side every single time.

Cartoon by Jerry King

"Why do I get the feeling my divorce is final?"

Photo by Nathan Gibson

My riding bud Phil Auldridge on his shiny new Indian.

Big Bend Loop

T he Big Bend[1] Loop is a simple way of taking a good look at one fourth of Texas, which is similar in distance to riding the circumference of forty-nine of the other fifty states. When you start out from Austin, located in Central Texas, you point your motorcycle due west for about 300 miles, hang a left, and ride south for 200 miles. These first 500 miles make up day one.

---

1   Big Bend National Park is spread across nearly 1 million acres of mountainous terrain on the border of Texas and Mexico. It's about the size of New Jersey, but the folks are more friendly.

On day two, you cross through the Big Bend National Park. Then you'll hug the Mexican border, heading east for a while and then south for a long time. Eventually, you'll find your way to Laredo. By day 3, you'll have made it to the southern tip of Texas on the edge of the Gulf of Mexico. On day 4, you can start meandering back to Austin, the 1,700-mile loop completed.

Day One
October 2016

Phil and I left at the absolute perfect time, for us. Daybreak is beautiful when you're riding a motorcycle due west. The sunrise crawls across your rearview mirrors for over an hour. Twilight evolves into shades of pink and blue until the main attraction rises up, a giant orange ball. Well, two orange balls if you count both rearview mirrors. It's really magical. That early in the morning, the first hour goes by fast. You'll be constantly watching for deer capable of causing an ugly unplanned stop. You find time to occasionally glance at the mirrors to enjoy the sunrise.

We rode the first 140 miles before making our first stop for fuel at the intersection of US 290 and I-10 West. As is the custom, Dorothee had loaded us up with homemade muffins, which we devoured with a McDonald's coffee. After that, it was a shit load of I-10. Normally we abide by the adage: Friends don't let Friends drive on the interstate. However, with the Big Bend Loop, there is no getting around it; we sucked it up and accepted one day of mindless 85 mph straight, eventless riding.

I made the mistake one time of taking a train from Perth, Australia, to Sydney without a sleeper car other than the bar car. This 50-hour, 2,000-mile experience put west Texas in perspective. The brush of west Texas reminded me of the outback. Fortunately, there is not near as much of the Texas sandbox as the Australian sandbox.

Our second stop, about 300 miles from Austin, would not have been memorable except for the butterflies. We found ourselves surrounded by thousands of them. It turns out we were crossing the migration pattern of yellow and orange monarch butterflies. They are beautiful to watch, until they cover your windshield and helmet shield with little orange and yellow splashes. I think this stop is when

I noticed an exhaust leak that was warming up my right calf.

Stop number three was in Fort Stockton, which is pretty much the armpit of the world—certainly the arm pit of Texas. This is where I discovered a little puddle of oil under my Harley. It seemed to be coming out about the middle of the forward cylinder. Harley guys take it for granted that you have a Harley dealership in any city large enough to get its name printed on the map. As it turns out, Fort Stockton should not be on the map. There wasn't a motorcycle repair shop of any description. I bought a $4.00 quart of oil for $20.00. Afterward, my Harley and I limped the 80 miles south to Alpine where a mechanic I had phoned said he would at least diagnose the issue.

I must add this: While I was in the parts store where I bought the extortion-priced oil, I noticed a picture of a very attractive, 21-year-old lady who was missing. She was last seen in Fort Stockton about a month before. After our tour of Fort Stockton, which had no noticeable redeeming characteristics, we formed the opinion that any 21-year-old with half a brain cell was going to go missing from Fort Stockton. That young lady probably jumped in the first truck she could convince to stop and was off to anywhere else!

We found the aforementioned dilapidated repair shop, Big Bend Motorcycles in Alpine, but there was no mechanic. He answered the phone right away when I called an hour and a half earlier from Fort Stockton, but he didn't answer any of my calls after that. With no other options, and given the leak didn't look as bad anymore, we had a two-beer lunch and pushed on.

The ride through the desert to Terlingua, Texas, was very nice, other than the constant worry that I was sitting on a potentially explosive motorcycle. When mountains started to pop up around us, the road began to take on some personality. Strangely, and to my delight, my Harley was no longer leaking oil by the time we stopped in Terlingua.

We passed a border patrol stop on the way, about 50 miles from the actual border. Because we were headed toward Mexico, we were not stopped, unlike those coming from the border. This is pretty much a non-issue unless you have contraband. It just so happened that I had a small amount of pot. It would go undetected, unless they had the dogs, and they usually have dogs. So, once we past the border patrol in Terlingua, Phil and I had to smoke up the evidence because tomorrow we would be going north again.

We treated ourselves to a strong bourbon and Coke, put a pretty good dent in my tiny pot supply, and went out to a nice meal of chicken fried boar at the Starlight Grill and Bar. At least, I think that's what we did.

Day Two
Big Bend Loop

If I omitted all the animal scares and fuel stop misadventures from day two, there would be little to write about. We departed our little no-tell-motel cabin at daybreak again. It's ill advised to ride early morning with limited visibility across the animal-invested mountains, but riding in the afternoon heat, which is 100+°F on average is also a bad idea. If you have charted a 500 mile day, you must strike a balance. Daybreak gives you some visibility with a somewhat early start.

We weren't 50 feet from dropping our keys in the return drop box when we noticed a kit fox on the side of the road. He was contemplating crossing the road in front of us. In the end, he had second thoughts, but we got a good look at him: bright eyes, very large ears, and a pointed nose. We weren't a mile down the road when a very large deer ventured out into the road directly in Phil's path. She managed to turn in time. Phil signaled to me that we should slow it down. Generally, deer don't come in herds of one. About 20 miles after Phil's close call, he crunched a rabbit and hated doing it. The next animal we came across was a large deer running down the side of the road about 10 feet from my right side mirror. We were traversing a cut in the mountain. As we approached the end of the cut, she had nowhere else to go. There was no real danger because I saw her in time, and she didn't bolt across the road. We didn't see another animal for 300 miles, but the last one we came across made up for it. There was a full-grown but very dead cow that had recently been hit by a car or (more likely) a truck. It was laying half on the road and half off. Driving at night is always a bad plan and we abstain from it.

My real concern was the Javelinas. I'd seen these short, pig-like animals running in herds on my last bike trip to Big Bend. They hang out in family groups of 20 to 50, are about 2 feet tall, and weigh around 50 lbs. They're very quick on their feet and not so quick in their brains. They have long, dagger-like teeth that hang out from under their snouts. They're basically miniature boars.

Photo by the Texas Parks & Wildlife Department

Javelinas are best observed at a distance.

Moving to the death by technology phase of our jaunt, Phil and I had disagreements with gas pumps at three separate stops on this day. When we pulled up to the pump, the *see attendant* alert was flashing on the display. Now, it's hot as hell; we'd already pulled up right against the pump, so I didn't have to get off the bike.

The last thing we wanted to do was park and go inside just for the opportunity to stand in line with a circus of rednecks buying cigarettes and lottery tickets. Technology makes me crazy when it doesn't work. I never know if it's a user error or the computer gods punishing me for being old.

In contrast to our technology dependent gas pumps, I had a much more pleasant experience in Indonesia while riding with my son a few years back. We simply pulled our rented bikes up to lemonade looking stand where a 12 year-old kid would fill our tanks from a used vodka bottle for not much money and clean our windshield...full service!

It was not all hassle. Everyone should ride Big Bend National Park at sunrise. The explosion of light from the sun on all the different mountain ranges and canyons is truly a spiritual experience. The colors change by the second and the pristine air puts a delightful coating on your nostrils and throat. That experience was exhilarating.

Once out of the mountain ranges and after the sun was high in the sky, there was a boat load of long flat highway running through wasteland more akin to the face of the moon than tillable terrain. On the upside, the speed limit was normally 75 mph, giving us 85 mph, and there were no towns to go through. Needless to say, if we got an opportunity to argue with a gas pump, we took it.

Our destination for the night was Hotel La Posada on the banks of the Rio Grande. It is one block from a border crossing. You can be in Mexico by foot in 15 minutes. I like the hotel but the real reason for choosing it is security for the motorcycles. The La Posada has underground parking and 24/7 security. You come through the garage door and show your hotel key to a guy with a big gun, or you do not enter the parking garage. Unattended motorcycles have a way of growing legs when parked in border towns.

I had planned to walk across the bridge to Mexico when we arrived (before dark only) into Nueva Laredo which is known to be more controlled by the Zetas than the police. In fact, the police have given up or have been bought off by the drug lords, leaving the Mexican army in open warfare with the Zetas and other drug cartels. I had suggested to Phil that he should bring his passport so we could walk across. We might even get to see a shooting! I should have left off the part about the shooting as Phil definitely did not bring his passport. In the not too distant past, nine tortured and murdered corpses had been found hanging from the very bridge we would be walking across. Phil may have made the right decision on this one.

We did go exploring right up until 7 p.m. in the deserted downtown area of Laredo looking for a restaurant. There was nothing open. Everything was closed. Laredo, a city of 250,000 and Nueva Laredo on the Mexican side, population 400,000, are now ghost towns after 4 p.m. due to the drug wars. One report said they were ghost towns and the ghosts are very dangerous.

We retired back to the security of our hotel

and had a very nice meal in their relatively expensive and relatively safe restaurant. After which and with little choice, we called it a night.

Day Three
The Texas Loop

Quite by accident, as opposed to strategy, Day 3 was a short ride. In hindsight, it was pure genius. South Padre Island is beautiful and The Pearl, our beach hotel, is by far the most luxurious place we have stayed. Turns out Phil has friends in both high and low places. His high-place friend is a VP Sales for Omni who got us in there for $69.00 a room. Phil brought his low-place friend with him—Yea!

Our experience back in Laredo was only a pleasant one because we did have a pretty decent hotel with very good security. Initially, I booked it because of the security for the motorcycles but the more we got to know Laredo, the more we appreciated the security of the La Posada for ourselves.

We fueled up first thing in the morning, still in the city. Phil said, "I am glad to be leaving Laredo."

I looked around at what I could see from the

dilapidated gas station with a lot of panhandlers and replied, "We're not out of here yet". As if it heard us, Laredo tried to sabotage our ride back. The damn pump wouldn't take our cards, and the attendant had the personality of a prison warden. He required us to leave our cards with him while we fueled up. Phil observed that we would likely see Nuevo Laredo charges on the cards from Rosie's Whorehouse. I hoped not, but he could have been right.

For the first 1,000 miles, we only saw two highway patrol cars, both near Fort Stockton on I-10. Previously, I had gotten exactly two tickets on I-10. Both near Fort Stockton.

Fifty miles outside of McAllen, we started to see highway patrol cars concealed behind every bush and tree. I stopped counting at 20. Business was good for them. This was a textbook speed trap. The speed limits vacillated between 55, 65, and 75 back and forth with no obvious change in congestion.

I thought this was very strange until I got an interesting clue to the mystery as we approached McAllen. I spotted a large red brick building marked "Texas Highway Patrol Training Academy", so the last 50 miles of our trip that day was a speed trap designed to train our uniformed public servants. Fortunately, we managed to avoid parcticipation in this training program. Phil always rides in front and did a good job of watching the continuously changing speed limits keeping us at the limit +5 and out of trouble.

We landed on South Padre Island to the sound of waves crashing on the beach and quickly found a place to have a drink overlooking the ocean. We followed that up with a wonderful meal of fresh red snapper and shrimp. Life is good.

Day Four
Big Bend Loop

How very simple life would be
If only there were two of me
A Restless Me to drift and roam
A Quiet Me to stay at home
A Searching One to find his fill
Of varied skies and newfound thrill
While sane and homely things are done
By the domestic Other One.

Excerpt: "The Double Life" by Don Blanding

If you haven't read "The Double Life" by Don

Blanding, Google it and have a read. It's one of my favorites. This passage captures the reason that return trips are bittersweet. I miss Susie and Jasper and the comforts of home, but it sure is nice to wander.

Our last day on the road was uneventful, or I should say it was nothing to write home about. We did stumble upon the best breakfast place of the trip: a Mexican mom and pop. Beyond that, Phil kept us off the interstate for the 400-mile trek back.

I'd like to close out the oil leak mystery from the beginning of this story: It remains a mystery. Our best guess is that I overfilled the oil when I changed it before the trip.

I was home only one night (to get my clothes washed) before I loaded Susie on the back of the Harley and headed to Natchitoches, Louisiana. That beautiful little town, about 400 miles from Austin, is the subject of the story "Going Back in Time." Right on the heels of the long and exciting Big Bend loop trip, Susie and I saddled up the Harley and headed out on another adventure.

Never pull up to stop directly behind the car in front of you. When your rearview mirror is reflecting a soccer mom coming at your ass like Leroy on a rocket in an SUV while on the phone, yelling at the kids and applying her third coat of mascara, you are going to want a place to go.

"What do you mean you were having so much fun riding with your buddies you lost track of time? You were supposed to be home over a year ago!

LADY MUST HAVE LOST HER SHIRT IN A CARD GAME

I have a very good photo of this couple at Sturgis and would love to use it. However, I do not know who they are and have no way of asking permission. The rule is that you cannot publish a photo, even when taken in public, if people are identifiable. We could have easily blurred their faces and printed it legally, but even with a blurred face, I could pick her out of a line up. If this is you, please come forward and give me permission, so I can get the real photo (which is great) in the re-print!

Sturgis Or Bust

I was nervous about riding in the dark for the first hour after a 5 a.m. departure. Hauling ass on narrow, crooked, deer-infested hill country roads in total darkness is of suspect judgement. I was very focused by necessity. Departing an hour later would have us making up that time in 100 degree plus Texas afternoon heat. Desperate men do desperate, and sometimes stupid, things.

We wisely decided to make the 1,421-mile run to Sturgis in three easy days, as opposed to two long days. Also, Phil and I share a conviction that friends do not let friends drive on the Interstate. We agree that life begins on the off-ramp. We also believe that hotels are places where you spend the night, not a fortune. At $40 for a downtown Amarillo, Texas room, the Civic Motel qualified! I will be kind and say the neighborhood was a bit shady. Of course, the coffee pot had long since been stolen, probably the same folks who took the sink. The next day I was up before daylight, but afraid to go looking for coffee because I had left my gun in Austin.

Noteworthy from the 500 mile ride the previous day were the curvy, Hill Country roads that spread across hundreds of miles. Best described as straight, flat nothing. These long stretches were punctuated by little towns with grand old county court houses, miles of giant wind mills, and cotton and sun flower fields. Did I mention the oil jacks pumping away, and the fumes of the crude oil blending with the cow shit smell of the stock yards? The panhandle grows energy, but not without an unmistakable fragrance!

We stopped for fuel in Post, Texas. The single redeeming characteristic of Post is that it makes a person eternally grateful to be living anywhere else.

My first employer in Virginia had a textile plant in Post and garnished considerable performance mileage by threatening to send low performing managers to Post, Texas as a developmental transfer. Said managers tended to get their act together when presented with this alternate opportunity.

At six the next morning it was dark, but nice and cool, so we shot out across the high desert plains in the moonlight. The sun poked its head out to our right about the time we started our descent into a cloud of fog that reduced visibility to about 25 feet. We slowed to a crawl, half afraid of being hit by a truck, or hitting someone who had neglected to turn their lights on.

Suddenly the fog lifted, but only by about 12 feet. It was mystical! You could reach out and touch the orange from the sun—we were a part of the sunrise for several miles. Then, as the elevation dropped, we were again in a thick fog with almost no visibility for about 50 miles. Complicating things was the fact that the thick fog made our windshields soupy, making it difficult to see, not to mention drenching our clothes. The first three hours of day two were not relaxing.

There are drunk riders.
There are old riders.
There are no old, drunk riders.

About the time we reached the cattle town of Dumas, Texas (pronounced *dumb-ass*), the sun was bright, but the air was definitely not clear. We only thought we smelled cow shit in Post, Texas. It was feed lot after feed lot! The town reeked of cow shit—not just a part of the town, but miles before and miles after. Unbelievable! We tied our bandanas over our faces, but to no avail. We looked for a pawn shop where we could trade our helmets in for gas masks, but there were none to be found. I refuse to ride through Dumas again without wearing scuba mask and an oxygen tank.

The next town was Kit Carson, Colorado, with a population of about 1400. We needed gasoline but there was only a closed gas station. Fortunately, the pumps worked if you had a credit card and did not care about pricing, but the station had been closed for years. Very strange!

Keep in mind that these cities all look alike and are about 125 miles apart with lots of open plains between. So if you have a problem, it is definitely your problem. If you get a chance to buy gas or a beer, you buy it.

We searched for most of the day for just that—beer and gasoline. We had eaten a muffin in Amarillo at 5 a.m., and it was 7 p.m. before we found a joint where we could get both a burger and a beer. These conservative western towns made a considerable contribution toward my sobriety on this trip, and I did not appreciate it one bit.

I cannot say enough about the scenery and the wealth you feel when traveling through the breadbasket states of Oklahoma and Missouri. So much lush land and productivity of corn, wheat, and cattle; feeding America and much of the rest of the world. There are also hundreds of miles of nothing, nothing but beauty…

stone formations and really big sky. Your mind wanders to what the first settlers must have seen and how they traversed this rough but scenic land without a motorcycle.

About 200 miles into Colorado, something worth mentioning happened at a coffee stop. It was time to shed my jacket. I stooped over to put it in my saddle bag, not realizing that I was too close to Main Street and my butt was well into the traffic zone. I heard Phil scream, "Nathan, Nathan!" I looked up to see a lady hitting her brakes and swerving to avoid hitting me. Yep, almost got my ass run over. I can see the obituary now: Nathan Gibson, self-proclaimed motorcycle safety expert, killed in an "almost motorcycle" accident. Got his ass run over, but fortunately his motorcycle was unharmed!

We made a short diversion to the not-so-historic site of "Carhenge," a spinoff on Stonehenge, of course.

Photo by Phil Auldridge

The design is a take on Stonehenge in the U.K.

Some crazy planted a dozen '50s, '60s, and '70s cars in the dirt in the image of Stonehenge, and alongside it a store selling overpriced t-shirts and making a fortune. He did pick some pretty cool cars—a '56 Cadillac, a Rambler Gremlin, a '61 Dodge Dart—and a number of cars that are a bit unusual, and now enshrined. The original Stonehenge was put together by religious crazies about 1500 years B.C. Their leaders did it to give the tribe a sense of purpose, but more to obligate the next generation to continue working to fulfill the obligation. Very large churches are built today for the same purpose.

Photo by Phil Auldridge

Carhenge enshrines 60's and 70's American-made cars.

By the third day we were riding in cool weather and at 4000 feet elevation, and it felt great. As we approached the Black Hills National Park, we stopped to get maps and stretch our legs at a welcome center. A lady park ranger told us that there were six motorcycle fatalities the day before, the first day of the Sturgis 75th anniversary rally. I made a mental note to avoid that for myself, as I know for sure the company I retired from will stop my pension if I get killed.

Then we were off, driving through scenery much different from the high plains desert we had seen before entering the Black Hills National Park. Motorcycles were ubiquitous. The Black Hills are just that. The type of fir tree there is very dark, and any random cloud in the sky casts a shadow that lays black on the thick forest.

Non-riders do not appreciate that riding is the same as yoga. You sit in one position and think of only one thing. The mind pushes out unimportant things, providing clarity and focus. Many folks sit behind desks with their busy minds driving them nuts with an endless list of uncompleted trivia. The disciplined motorcycle guy does not lose focus and gets safely to his or her destination feeling relaxed. The most disciplined office professional gets home feeling very stressed and needing a drink.

The craziness in the town of Sturgis was supposed to be the main event. I did enjoy it thoroughly, but the old adage about it being more about the journey and less about the destination was validated. The trek up and back easily trumps one day of loud noise and loud people trying to sell you overpriced motorcycle accessories.

Sturgis is 50 miles from where we stayed in Sundance, population 1222. No stop lights, one restaurant, and one drug store that closes at noon on Saturdays. It was very peaceful and a good place to land. We shoved off for the craziness of Sturgis at 7 a.m., arriving about 7:45 a.m. and finding a few thousand bikes there already.

We saw an eccentric old guy (about our age and level of eccentricity) show up on a loud, short, plump bike (a Buell) about the time we arrived. The guy had a goatee, was bald, and had a beer belly from hell. He hit the breakfast restaurant door just behind us and was vying for a booth along with us...loads of people there, even that early. Well, we ended up sharing a booth with him. Turns out he was a piece of work even by our standards. A retired firefighter, now a vendor of leather motorcycle leggings designed to protect your calves. He talked non-stop, having perfected the art of breathing through his ears, trying to sell us on these things with a beginning price of $175. I felt like I had breakfast with an infomercial. He did pick up the entire tab, so all's well that ends well. After breakfast it was largely people watching and motorcycle gawking.

This was very early in the morning, sparse compared to the number of cycles that would come later in the day. Attendance was projected to be 1 million!

Phil was hell-bent on not leaving Sturgis empty handed, which means he was looking for free stuff. We filled out electronic forms on kiosks with made up addresses and false phone numbers. We were rewarded with free t-shirts, without worrying about being contacted later to buy their wares.

Toward the end of the trip, I actually got Phil a free Bible to add to his saddlebag full of free stuff (although I suspect the Bible did not make it out of Sturgis). At one stop he only got a cheap ball point pen, which licked all the red off his lollipop; thought he was going to cry.

We did tour the Sturgis motorcycle museum on Main Street, and it was very well done. It had some Enfields and old BSAs and Triumphs mixed in with the Harleys that you knew would be there. It took me down memory lane a bit, with some old Cushman motor scooters and my favorite, a 1969 Honda 305. It was the cycle of my dreams as a teenager, but one that I could not afford back then.

There was a black cloud in the distance by 3 p.m., and we had enjoyed more than enough of Sturgis. We should have left at 2 p.m. We hit the front about 15 miles out of Sturgis, and the gentle rain quickly deteriorated into high winds, very heavy rain, crashing lightning, and (saving the best for last) half-inch hail. Fortunately, we were able to pack in with a dozen other bikers under an overpass. We hung out there, with large trucks periodically showering us with dirty road water, until the rain slowed. As it turns out, we left there too early, and the heavy rain returned. We made it to the hotel drenched, but pretty happy that we had checked off the Sturgis rally day and could ride the beautiful Black Hills once again.

Within minutes of our return, we were in the hotel hot tub with a Jack Daniels and Coke, and the rough weather was a distant, bad dream. After another Jack and Coke, the ride back seemed a well-planned adventure; another inadvertent stroke of genius on our part.

The grand plan the following day was for a 7:30 a.m. departure, and to hit a number of popular sites in the Black Forest National Park. The problem was that the fog was so thick we could not see across the motel parking lot, and the weather forecast called for a 40 percent chance of severe thunderstorms in southwestern South Dakota…which is exactly where our ride plan took us. We decided to lollygag and wait and see. Phil had his eye on a coffee shop/ restaurant that opened at 7:30 am. They served high-end lattes and possibly bagels. You have to keep in mind that Phil would just as soon live off of fancy new-fangled lattes and lemon meringue pies. He even threatened to order me a latte. That scared me to death, as I feared I would suddenly start speaking Californian. I was saved by the calendar, as this yuppie place was not open on Sundays. We ended up at a somewhat conservative mom and pop place that had normal coffee and somewhat normal food. But their advertised ham was off by one letter. It was definitely Spam, not ham.

> There's something ugly about a *new* bike on a trailer.

We had a splendid ride through the Black Hills, complete with very curvy roads and waterfalls and a river that flowed beside the road most of the time. The red limestone mountains that leaped from the valleys were magnificent and just breathtaking. The curves were sharp and continuous and the rain never came!

We headed back to Texas, but did detour through Sturgis one more time to see what it looked like without the rally. As expected, it is just a sleepy little South Dakota town for 51 weeks out of the year. We again elected to make the trek back in three days instead of two. We also modified the route so as not to see the same things going back.

Our last day of the ride was supposed to be a short day, but then things do not always go as planned. We departed at dawn, but within a couple of hours the sprinkles turned into some fairly serious rain. Phil spotted a closed gas station as a place to get in out of the weather. Then something magical happened. We got a lesson in Kansas agriculture! Only 50 yards from us was an obscure little restaurant. We walked over and, sure enough, it was open. The old man in there (about our age), Willard, was just fixing himself breakfast. He offered to pour us a cup of coffee. He also poured out his life circumstance, which was very interesting and, quite frankly, touching. Seems the owner, his sixty-something-year-old girlfriend Ruth, owned the place and had been running it for 35 years. Her husband died about 14 years ago. Willard had "taken up with her" seven years ago. Seems they knew each other because his son had married her daughter, and because of this they shared three grandchildren. Neither had ever lived anywhere else other than this 333-person wide place in the road. He was a farmer. He was very open about the bushels of wheat, bushels of corn, and so forth and the impact of the weather on the crops and the prices he got and the expenses. It did not take us long to figure out that he made about $15,000 a year in the good years, and lost about the same amount in the bad years. In the restaurant, Ruth was pretty much killing herself for nothing, and Willard was pretty much killing himself for nothing in the fields.

They had each other and covered the backs of their neighbors and seemed to be pretty happy, and very happy to have the ear of two old geezers like us to talk to.

The clouds did not part, but they got as good as they were going to get. We hit the road hoping for the best. Most of the heavy stuff was gone and we made good time. The roads were straight and the scenery did not change much; beautiful, but no trees. Occasionally, we saw a tree and would stop to take a picture of it. We suspected some rich land owner had planted an artificial tree just to mess with us.

Coming back home is always bittersweet. Back to the list of things we do that is our life. Back to reality, baby. On the road with all you need for a week (which is all you need for a lifetime as well) packed in a small bag is about as carefree as it gets. Your job is merely staying alive and enjoying the camino!

We saw some very strange things. Believe it or not, we saw grown men pulling trailers with perfectly good and functional motorcycles on them…and this to a motorcycle event. I have not seen Sturgis billed as a trailer event. Maybe I did not get the e-mail. If you ever see one of my motorcycles on a trailer, please call 911 because it has been stolen.

We also saw a young woman who must have been in a card game the night before, because

she had definitely lost her shirt. There were quite
a few women in the same game apparently, but
no one was taking pictures of them.

Photo by Nathan Gibson

This old steel bridge is just one example of
something you do not see when traveling
on the interstate.

Tragically, this Sturgis event took the record
for most fatalities; there were 12. The other
record was the number of bikes attending.

News agencies have reported that one
million parcticipants showed up for the 75th

anniversary. I am a little surprised there were not more fatalities. The skill level I observed was scary. The fact that there were a large number of folks trailering their bikes from within the state, as well as bordering states, should tell you something. If you cannot ride your bike a few hundred miles to the event, you might be inexperienced. We had an awesome ride, saw some breathtaking scenery, and were smart enough to plan our weeklong Sturgis trip to be six hours in Sturgis at the rally…and the rest of the time riding.

Photo by Phil Auldridge

One of the many morning sunrises.

"HERBIE, SAFE SEX IS NOT MAKING
LOVE WITH YOUR HELMET ON."

They's a Woman In That Room

G ot a noon start out of Spartanburg. I needed a 750-mile day but it wasn't in the cards. A major blowout on the truck I was only seconds from passing set the tone for this adrenaline laden leg from Spartanburg, S.C. to Meridian, Mississippi. The truck driver over-braked and swerved into the I-26 median, I dodged the debris freed from his trailer when it overturned, while UPS truck driver on my right did a hell of a job in order to avoid killing me. Just another Sunday afternoon bike ride, so far.

Flooding precipitated by the first hurricane of the season was Murphy's second attack. The driving rain was laying the bike to a 30 degree slant while the passing tractor trailer trucks were providing a solid wall of water, my own private tsunami. Visibility was intermittently poor to zero. Periodically, I would get lucky; when multiple lightning strikes would improve visibility. Oh joy!

But the fun had not started yet. It was an incompetent but innocent mistake. The no-tell, hotel clerk at the Super 8 assigned me a room already occupied—by a rough group of Harley bikers. They did not look parcticularly yuppie-friendly. They were lined up sitting in plastic chairs on the walkway drinking Jack Daniels out of paper cups when I strolled up in my sandals and parachute pants.

Hey, I thought they would like my '06' BMW snuggled close in between their hogs. Surely, they had been trained in the value of diversity at one of the South Alabama cultural centers. I was delighted that my assigned room, #110, was directly behind this sidewalk happy hour.

Innocently, perhaps naively, I slid my key into the door nearest them. From behind, I hear "They's a woman in bed in that room," coming from a large bearded tattoo with a loud raspy voice. I turned to show this fine gentleman my hotel room 110 envelope, when to my amazement and to his, I blurted out "that's great!" and laughed. I sensed immediately that he did not appreciate the humor and that the woman in the room was likely his main squeeze, or more likely, "their" main squeeze.

> Young riders pick a destination.
> Old riders pick a direction.

He approached me with some haste, at which time I got more serious about showing him the envelope, deploying my best southern redneck accent to explain the hotel clerk's mistake. His friends thought it was hellaciously funny. Their laughter helped diffuse the situation.

I did get a peek inside the room. I saw either a very large woman under a sheet or else someone was trying to hide a U-Haul trailer under a circus tent.

Through very heavy weather, dodging airborne blown-out tires and swerving trucks, this incident was the most serious near-miss of the day. The talking tattoo saved my life. "The woman in bed in that room" would have killed me for sure.

Riding in an automobile's blind spot is extremely dangerous. Minimize your time spent where the motorist cannot see you by mirror. Auto drivers do not turn their heads as if it is against their religion. Either nail the gas, or slow down, but do not camp out in a vehicle's blind spot unless organ donation is high on your bucket list.

Cartoon by Jerry King

"No offense, but after building that bike for over three years, I thought you would've made better progress."

Speeding Ticket, Anyone?

I n many states there are about as many warning tickets given out as actual tickets. The ratio varies widely by officer and by location. If you are more than 10 mph over, your odds of getting a warning are slim. However, the way you handle yourself could get you a write-down to a speed allowing you to take defensive driving for a dismissal. The officer has 100 percent discretion in writing you a warning versus a real point-toting ticket. The hassle factor between the two is huge. Take my advice: make it an easy stop for the officer.

1. Pull over quickly.
2. Remain on the bike with your hands on the grips.
3. Do not scramble through your tank bag for your credentials.
4. Do not speak until spoken to.
5. Follow instructions and be polite.
6. Do not tell funny stories or provide excuses. They've heard them all.
7. Do not admit or deny guilt. Simply acknowledge that you understand what the officer is saying.

Note: If your record is clean, you can point that out. The officer has probably run your plates already and knows if you are a virgin or not before walking up to your bike.

Remember: Nothing works all the time or with all the officers. Practice makes perfect!

Although I gave you a list of actions you can take to ensure you've done everything possible to make it an easy stop for the officer, the best way to avoid a ticket is to hold your speed to no higher than 10 mph over the posted limit. Unless you're in a school zone or in Lakeway, Texas, they'll normally let you have it. They give you 5 mph, and you take five. However, when you take six or more in addition to the five they give you, sooner or later, you are going to meet a new friend complete with documentation. If you meet a new friend, you can sometimes negotiate a warning. In my experience, total and unabashed honesty is the best policy:

> "Officer, I knew the speed limit, I do not have an emergency, I am aware of the safety risk I am imposing on myself and others, and if you would be so kind as to consider a warning ticket, I will get my act together."

At least for today.

> Bikes parked out front mean cold beer and good chicken fried steak.

If in England you can try this—it worked once for me:

> "Officer, over 200 years ago you guys rounded up your prisoners, your paupers, and your misfits and shipped them to America. I am a product of that gene pool. Is it really fair to expect me to follow rules?"

In the States, you might try:

> "Officer, I was pushing to get a little ahead of you because my ex-wife ran off with a trooper and I was terrified that you were bringing her back."

In truth, I can only tell you what not to do in regard to parking tickets. A few years back three buddies and I packed our camping gear and rode from Austin to Sturgis, South Dakota, for the infamous biker rally. On the third day, we went out for breakfast very early. Even at that hour, the parking lot was full, so we backed our bikes into the most convenient illegal parking space clearly marked as a fire lane. After breakfast, we headed back to our bikes as an officer was just finishing writing us a ticket. He handed it to me and said, "You can split this with your friends."

Following instructions to a *T*, I proceeded to fold the ticket perfectly in half and ripped it in two. I then took both of the halves and ripped them in two. Now having four pieces, I handed them out. "Ken, this is your share, Bob, this is yours," and so forth. It turned out that the officer had no sense of humor and, in fact, was so underwhelmed with my creativity that he proceeded to write four brand-new tickets vs. the one, one for each of us. This did not endear me to my buds.

In the aforementioned parking ticket example, you can see that it is also possible to talk yourself into a ticket. Once while zipping along I-35 on my '93 Harley police bike, I got pulled over by an officer also on a Harley police bike. He happened to be a black guy and I happen to be a white guy. Well, as usual, he asked if I knew why he had pulled me over. To be honest, I really didn't know. I mean, I was running less than 10 over the posted limit.

Why I blurted out my next thought is still a

mystery to me. Maybe my brain had a smartass fart, but this creative one-liner certainly earned me a ticket:

Officer
"Do you know why I
pulled you over today, sir?

Me
"Don't tell me. Let me
guess. Racial profiling?"

The moral of the story is twofold. One, you can talk yourself into a ticket. Two, it is not mandatory to verbalize every thought that you have.

Cartoon by Jerry King

"I'm just curious, which one of you was dropped off by their boyfriend on a really fast motorcycle?"

"WE ONLY NEED THE ROOM FOR AN HOUR."

The Tail Of The Dragon

By way of introduction, with its 318 sharp turns in just 11 miles, the narrow and crooked Tail of the Dragon is a dream ride and should be on every avid rider's bucket list.

Designated as U.S. Route 129, The Tail coils between the Cherokee National Forest to the West and the Great Smoky Mountains to the East. Route 129 begins at the Georgia-North Carolina border and certainly doesn't run northwest as the crow flies, unless the crow is drunk. There are no intersecting roads or driveways to hamper your creativity on hundreds of scenic twists. Obviously, as a public road, it has traffic traveling both ways. Just imagine the Daytona 500 with cars traveling in both directions at insane speeds.

I typically ride by myself, or preferably, with Susie Q. hanging on to me. I am not a joiner of groups, gangs, or clubs. Not unlike Frank Sinatra, I like to do it my way.

Having said that, when you do come across a compatible riding pal, it is a genuine treasure. I eliminate a lot of potential riding buds due to my inclination for

1. early starts
2. calling it a day by 6 p.m.
3. running it up over 100 mph (as needed)

Or perhaps it's my charming personality that shortens my list of potential riding partners, but then I digress.

My friends, Phil and David, remain extremely compatible riding buds. You met Phil in

"Sturgis or Bust," "Big Bend Loop," and "Going Back in Time." David was my riding mate in "North to Alaska" and on this trip to The Tail. It started out innocently enough but, just to be honest, the trip was David's fault.

The only good view of a thunderstorm is in your rearview mirror

We were hanging out on a Sunday evening having a burger when, out of nowhere, David asked if I had ever ridden the Tail of the Dragon. I said, "No, but I've read about it and would like to give it a go sometime."

David replied, "Can you leave in the morning?"

I couldn't help myself. I replied, "David, I can leave tonight!" David met me at my house at 7 a.m. sharp the next morning. Some folks likely plan their trips a little further in advance, but at our age, you best get on with it.

The Tail is 1,096 miles Northeast of Austin, Texas, situated near the state lines of Tennessee, North Carolina, and Georgia. We ran hard and fast with minimal stops and bit off 798 miles of the trip on the first day.

We compromised on the hotel as David leans more toward the Hilton, while Motel 6 is just fine with me. I try to get to the check-in desk before David, so I can haggle over discounts without him whining about thread counts and room services available. I find his list of required amenities very strange given we were both raised by blue collar families in small, southern, conservative towns. Perhaps David picked up a stray gene from some distant aristocratic ancestor.

On day two, we got an early start and knocked out the last 300 miles before noon. The ride began to get crooked and beautiful well before we reached Robbinsville, North Carolina, which would be our home for the night. Despite its population of only 607, motorcycles were swarming around Robbinsville like honeybees to a hive.

Our compromise hotel for the night was a Double Tree with a lobby filled with bikers. Leathers, helmets, and beards adorned these large, walking tattoos. Now, I am of average height and build while David is a very large man: 6 feet and 4 inches. He's not fat, but thick, with a booming voice that compliments his quick wit.

Before you ask, yes, I did beat David to the counter and was hot into negotiations when he caught up with me. The lady behind the check-in counter was asking me how long we needed the room. Before I could respond, David looked at her, put his arm around me, and said, "Honey, we only need a couple hours!"

The lobby went quiet with all eyes and sneers upon us. *Holy shit, David! Why'd you do that?* I pulled out my credit card as fast as I could, got my plastic key, and bolted for my room— still four shades of crimson.

Next day, the ride was exhilarating. I would love to describe it to you, but I cannot do that anymore than I could describe the taste of a chocolate chip cookie. We ran the circuit fast and furious on the first lap, coming back for the next at a slower, touristy pace. This time we stopped at overlooks that gazed out over the valleys made by the Great Smoky Mountains. The view served as a great backdrop while we chatted it up with fellow bikers from all over the United States.

The next morning, we ran The Tail one more time before heading for the Blue Ridge Parkway, only an hour away. Toward the end of that last challenging ride on The Tail, I came very near to losing it on a deceivingly innocent-looking curve.

The state had recently mowed the roadside grass, leaving trimmings on the shoulder. I'm not sure if you've heard, but a quarter inch of grass covering a road surface is as slick as owl shit. I didn't go down, but it was the closest I've ever been to going down without going down. Just another lesson not learned, I suppose.

With a fresh shot of adrenaline to wake me up, we headed for the Blue Ridge Parkway. We thought The Tail was the main event. Little did we know, the Blue Ridge Parkway can be a spiritual experience if traveled on a spring morning with the clouds settling in below us but above the treetops. Those clouds gave the Smokies their name.

In some places, the spruce stuck their heads out. The clouds cleared at times, and you could see miles of rich valleys and distant, shining streams so blue they seemed an outlet from the sky. The shapes and shades of green were immeasurable. Zooming in, the wild flowers and blooming trees put on quite a show both in beauty and aroma. The road was isolated, and although the speed limit was 45 mph, we drove much slower and stopped frequently.

At 469 miles long, the Blue Ridge Parkway is America's longest linear park. The Parkway runs through 29 North Carolina and Virginia counties, beginning very near the point where Tennessee, North Carolina, and Georgia touch.

Reluctantly, I peeled off toward South Carolina while David continued along the parkway. I was meeting friends with whom I had worked 15 years before, while David continued well into Virginia over the next couple of days. The grand plan was for us to meet three days later in Knoxville, Tennessee, at mid-day and ride together, stopping near Memphis for the night. Then we would take on the 650 mile ride into Austin.

Have I mentioned that David is not a sane man? He passed through Knoxville from somewhere near D.C. two hours before our agreed upon rendezvous. He left me a message that said he was headed for Texas, which I thought was a joke. Austin was 1,038 miles down the road from Knoxville, and he had already been riding for a half a day.

By the time I got to Memphis, he had left me a delirious voice mail from Texarkana singing, "The Yellow Rose of Texas." He talked about getting laid, and all the other great things Kay was going to do for him when he got back home to Austin. At this point, I was seriously worried about him. I hoped he had grabbed a room in Texarkana and was pulling my chain. He wasn't. That fool rode right through to Austin, putting well over 1,500 miles behind him in one day.

There is a well-known achievement in the motorcycle world called the Iron Butt Award. This is awarded to those riding over 1,000 miles in any one 24-hour period. I have my patch, and I understand the temptation, kind of. However, riding more than 1,500 miles in 21 hours deserves a whole new level of recognition. I'm thinking we should call it The Dumb Ass Award!

What is in front of you is less than half of your problem. The bigger devil may be behind you. A motorcycle can go from 60 mph to a complete stop in 2.5 seconds, 134 feet. A car takes 4.5 seconds, 271 feet to stop at 60 mph. If a car is on your ass and you stop for a hazard as fast as you can you are going to get some time off work and brand new bandage outfit or worse.

"BUT OFFICER, I WASN'T TALKING ON A CELL PHONE."

Sorry, I Almost Killed You

I lived near Oxford, England for 3 years before retiring back to Lake Travis. Once past the round-a-bouts and driving on the other side of the road, I found driving *much* safer there. Two differences stood out which, if adopted in Lakeway, would save lives and reduce congestion.

One, the English are forbidden and fined if caught doing anything other than driving with both hands on the wheel and their eyes on the road. It barely made the third page news in the London Times when a lady lost her license for one year after being caught combing her hair while driving down the M-1 (4 lanes each way). One never observes drinking coffee or hand-held cell phones when driving there. These are against the law and absolutely culturally unacceptable. This law is enforced.

Second, the English abide by a law (one we share but ignore) that says the inside lane is for passing. If not passing, *move right*. This allows those wishing to drive the speed limit to do so without passing using the outside lane, thereby avoiding dangerous lane changes. Even the third world country of Oklahoma sometimes enforces this law. This law, if enforced, would reduce the number of cars on the road at any one time, i.e. reduce congestion.

This brings me to my story where a nice lady in Lakeway tried to kill me this week. I ride my BMW motorcycle inside the 50 mph speed zone on 620 in Lakeway about twice a day. I set the cruise control on 50 mph in order to avoid getting acquainted with one of Lakeway's dedicated, diligent and hardworking uniformed public servants. They do a nice job and are busy meeting new friends almost every time I pass through. But I digress.

This 'would be' assailant was driving a new white Toyota Solara. She was wallowing in the inside lane using all 15 feet of the lane with her 8 foot wide car. She was obviously on her cell and driving about 10 miles under the speed limit. About 10 of us were lined up behind her wanting to drive the 50 mph speed limit. I cautiously moved to the right lane to pass when her car wandered, without a turn signal, into my lane. My cycle has a horn like a freight train. I laid on it and evaded to the right of the right lane — she jerked her steering wheel and swerved back into the "passing" lane that she had hogged for 3 miles.

Here is the punch line! I pulled up beside her passenger window and glared at her. She mouthed, while pointing to her cell, "I was using my cell phone," as if this was a perfectly good reason to block off 620 and nearly kill a cyclist.

Well excuuuuse me! How impolite of me to interrupt your phone call for a pedicure appointment at De Vinci's Spa just because I needed to go to the post office!

You go where you are looking. Look down and your ass is going down. Look only where you really want to go just like you do when you are at the beach!

"But tonight is going to be romantic. We'll drink a bottle of wine while I work on my bike."

"I WAS NOT GAULKING, I WAS JUST CURIOUS!"

Dangerous Woman

C ars are a breed apart from motorcycles. We all know that. However, even while related, sidecar bikes are totally different animals than a normal bike. Sidecar bikes are neither cars nor bikes. Bikes and, to some extent, cars really want to travel in a straight line unless told otherwise. In stark contrast, a sidecar bike is neither symmetrical nor obedient.

When you brake, these vehicles hunt for a ditch to the left, as most of the braking power is on the left side of the bike. Acceleration sends this bike into a hard right turn in search of the ditch on the other side of the road. As opposed to operating under common motorcycle logic, these bikes are rabid, hunting for a ditch at all times.

Riding a normal bike is a full-time job; riding a sidecar bike is a full-time job, plus overtime. You are constantly adjusting course in order to stay alive, but you still have to manage all the ordinary hazards associated with bikes.

As we all know, an effortless weight shift will coax a normal bike into your desired direction. With a sidecar, you can forget about that shit. There is nothing effortless about a sidecar bike. It is not a relaxing ride; it is a cute ride and, with practice, even a fun ride. But forget relaxing, forget effortless.

The sidecar will come up from the road, cause your bike to tilt, and at a certain angle, will flip over and very likely kill you. I cannot tell you the degrees of the angle required to flip, or when it will happen to you. I have had my sidecar hover high enough above the pavement to scare the pee pee out of me. It happened when I least expected it, so be aware. There is no warning light to tell you a flip is coming, but trust me, it will get your undivided attention.

Getting a very heavy girlfriend, who is also dumb enough to ride in the sidecar, can minimize the chances of a flip. My girlfriend is neither heavy nor dumb, so I used sandbags until I rescued my dog, Jasper, who loves to ride in the sidecar.

Photo by Sherry Pye

Nathan with Jasper, who is wearing his doggles.

The closest I came to flipping my bike was in Lakeway, Texas, and it was a woman's fault. I was only going about 10 mph in a strip mall parking lot. The young lady at fault was walking from the Spa On Lake Travis to her BMW, wearing a pair of spandex shorts.

Well, let's not use the word *gawking*. Let's be kind and say I was curious. Because this dangerous woman distracted me, the right wheel on the sidecar slammed into a curb, sending the sidecar into a 45-degree angle. The young lady got a grin out of it. I got a bent wheel rim, a red face, and hopefully a safety lesson.

If you're just starting out, I strongly recommend you get lots of experience in a large, empty parking lot (away from health spas) before going on the road with a sidecar bike.

If you don't ride in the rain, you don't ride.

"You were going too slow, then you were going too fast. You hit every pothole and you're making the turns too wide. And another thing..."

"THANK YOU FOR SHARING THE SQUEEGEE."

Dirty Windshields Can Be Life Threatening

B   ut not in the way you might first think. I like to take a 6:30 a.m. walk in a quiet neighborhood about two miles from my home. When I headed out this morning, my windshield was so dirty I could hardly see through it, so I diverted about 600 yards to the Speedy Mart. I pulled up to the gas pumps, not needing gas but needing the water and a squeegee.

I was running a few minutes behind my normal schedule but had to clean the windshield or I could not drive into the sun. Holy shit, no squeegee. Someone had stolen the damn squeegee. I was irritated, to say the least.

I happened to look to the other side of the gas pumps, where a big, burly guy was on the other side of his SUV pumping gas. He was tall enough for me to see his head above the vehicle. For whatever reason, I blurted out, "Some asshole has taken the squeegee." He stared at me for a second then lumbered around his SUV and squeegeed off his back window. Holy shit, I had just called one of the biggest tattoos I have ever seen an asshole!

Taking his sweet time, he cleaned his back window, giving me some time to struggle for something charming to say. He finished, and then holding the squeegee started lumbering over with purpose and determination toward me. I was wondering if he was going to give me the squeegee or stick it up my ass. He had the look of a big redneck that had just been called an asshole by a small old fart.

Words were not coming too fast, but about the time he got within striking distance I made an attempt to recover by saying, "And you must be the nice gentleman who has the *other* squeegee."

He was not convinced that I had not called him an asshole, but he was a bit confused and unsure, so he gruffly shoved the squeegee in my general direction and tromped away. What a way to start your day!

New tires have a coating that makes them very slick for the first 25 miles or so. Before you start hot dogging it to check out your new rubber investment, take it very easy for the break-in period or the rubber might be more expensive than you think.

Going Back In Time

I must jump ahead in my little story to say that Natchitoches, Louisiana, is—hands down—the most beautiful small town in the United States that I have visited. It was the first city founded following the Louisiana Purchase from the French. Situated on the beautiful Cane River, Natchitoches is only 50 miles from the Louisiana-Texas state line. It's halfway between Shreveport and Baton Rouge, but it's nothing like either of those cities.

Hanging baskets line the cobblestoned

Front Street, with rows of quaint shops and restaurants. All these early 1900s stores on main street are river front. The scene reminds me of Victoria, Canada or Flores, France. The city's charm could be described as a concentrated version of Charleston, South Carolina. There is no junk to be seen here. We're visiting the third world country of Louisiana, so there is a high degree of probability that major junk is not too far away. However, this little town is truly a flower among thorns. Phil said it best, "It's like Disneyland or a movie set: Almost too perfect." To steal the famous quote by General MacArthur, "I shall return."

Phil initiated this motorcycle adventure (again), and I am indebted to him (again). Phil and I are both gainfully unemployed, but he seems to work harder at it and gets more done than me. He had survived a busy month and was ready to get the hell out of Dodge. Good riding weather had arrived; winter was only a few short months away. The road was beckoning. I had survived a steady regimen of my morning coffee, reading the Wall Street Journal, walking my dog, Jasper, and rounding up pool buddies for the afternoon games. I needed a break too!

We strategically dodged the morning traffic on Ranch Road 620 in our flight out of town. Not because we planned to leave later, but because the contractor to whom I handed my house off to was running an hour late. While waiting, we devoured delicious muffins that Phil's wife, Dorothee, had baked just that morning. How she puts some batter in the oven and makes it come out so moist—with the perfect amount of sweetness—is totally beyond me. Whatever magic she sprinkles in, she does it consistently, and I'm not complaining!

Before long, we were traveling between Round Rock and Taylor, passing an untold number of large, new, and nearly empty car lots. Who comes to this part of the world to buy cars? The answer is no one. These cars spend most of the year on their south Austin lots, wintering on these lots each year around December. All because, about 25 years ago, the city fathers of Austin invented an inventory tax to be imposed on car dealers in Travis County. The inventory tax is based on the amount of inventory in Travis County at the end of each calendar year. Not long after that, any dealership with half a brain cell bought cheap farmland in

Williamson County and established a new car lot. Then, like clockwork, every year around mid-December, 80 percent of the cars parked on I-35 South in Travis County magically migrate north to Highway 79, just inside Williamson County. For some reason, by mid-January the dealerships always needed the cars back on I-35 South. Amazing.

As I was saying, we found ourselves approaching the Taylor by-pass. For many of these small Texas towns, a by-pass is tax dollars well spent. For Taylor, to by-pass or not to by-pass is time-of-day dependent. Founded in 1949 and situated on Main Street, Louis Mueller's BBQ, smokes the best beef ribs in the world. Foodies never take the Taylor by-pass at lunchtime. As it was too early for lunch, we took the by-pass. The threat of driving through Taylor is good training for driving through the cities of Thorndale and Rockdale, both of which got stuck in the Great Depression and are still waiting for the New Deal. Once past these two eyesores, the views were uplifting. Pasture and small farms whipped past us on both sides: Black dirt and cedar trees turned to tillable land, hardwood trees, and pines.

The roads were good and the speed limits were tolerable at 70 mph and sometimes 75 mph, but those signs are subjective. The real limit is the posted speed limit plus 10 mph. The police give you 5 mph, and you take 5 mph. After that, you are likely to make a new uniformed friend.

We had only ridden 99 miles—and it wasn't even 11 a.m.—when we stopped for fuel. Forget that we had just eaten some delicious home baked muffins; Phil asked if it was too early for lunch. He followed this up by saying that we were approaching a mom and pop restaurant where he had once eaten the best chicken fried steak to be found. Phil is a foodie and does not pass out his compliments lightly. Of course we stopped, and oh dear, it was worth it.

Full of chicken fried steak, the ride between our pig-out brunch and our first afternoon beer stop was exhilarating. We pretty much had the road to ourselves. The scenery didn't change much, and we were delighted that it did not. The farmland rolled by, tree types blending together and changing at times. Why do certain trees prefer to live in certain areas? More importantly, why did 3 different species of cedar choose to live in the hill country where I live? I understand that when you are going up a mountain, the tree types vary with the changes in elevation; various types of hardwoods blanket the bottom, followed by cedars, then pines, firs, and different types of firs. It must be the soil of flat, east Texas. There you have it: Cedar trees must not need soil. The price of living on a rock is to have cedar allergies for three months out of the year.

About 145 miles from our chicken fried steak food orgy, Phil had another brilliant idea, "Is it too early to stop for a beer?"

In a town of about 15,000 people that looked otherwise progressive, there were no beer joints, only antique stores and churches. No wonder the citizens looked so grumpy! We would not give up, and eventually found a pretty nice Italian restaurant that had something that resembled a bar. The owner was the only one there, and was happy to see us. He didn't seem as happy that he had no other customers. I'm sure it didn't help that during his lunch rush, we only wanted a couple of beers. Our Italian beer stop was located less than 200 miles away from our destination.

The trip from Austin, Texas, to Natchitoches, Louisiana, is shorter than 400 miles. It was a short ride day but a perfect ride day. The experience transported us to another world. The first thing you see when riding into this fairyland town is the oldest university in the state of Louisiana. Universities are repositories of great knowledge. The best students from the best high schools bring a lot of knowledge into universities. Then they graduate, leave with no knowledge, and all the knowledge accumulates right there in the universities!

We took a short Natchitoches walking tour by the river, hoping to do a little menu research of riverside restaurants. After that, we found our no-tell motel across from the university. There must be a million little no-tell motels, and it is really hard for them to distinguish themselves, but this motel pulled it off. They found a 5-foot sloth[2] to run the front desk.

2   The three-fingered Sloth is the slowest animal in the world. The name sloth is actually a synonym of slow motion. The top speed of a sloth is 0.003 miles per hour. They are so slow that algae grows on them.

He was Indian—as in red dot camel jock Indian, of course—but a sloth he was, and a slow sloth at that! He had no obvious health issues, but his moves were slower than slow. He demonstrated smooth, deliberate, and slow motion like I have never seen achieved. He did a fine job, but his absence of speed was truly remarkable.

After the slowmo show in the lobby, we showered and headed off to a fabulous outside patio dinner overlooking the river. A perfect end to a splendid ride.

In keeping with the theme of this road trip, we got off the next day to a lazy 8 a.m. start. Why not? We hit the road, which included an across-the-river loop tour, traveling less than three miles before hitting a breakfast café that specializes in meat pies. We spent a leisurely hour at this quaint café, styled similarly to the early 1900s. More than half of that hour was spent looking for a waitress. We waited a while. Then Phil went on a waitress hunting expedition. He came back empty handed. I followed up, taking a look for myself. All I had to do was walk into the kitchen signed employees only. I asked the cook, "Does this restaurant come equipped with a waitstaff?"

A lady replied, "That would be me. I will come out when I have time." Eventually, she did.

I ordered the meat pie special, which was prominently advertised on the restaurant signage. As I waited for my meal, I imagined my order would be similar to a deep, savory chicken potpie complete with a slit in the crust on top. The meat pie that landed on the table in front of me looked more like an apple turnover, except with a thicker and much heavier deep-fried crust. It came with rather spicy and greasy ground beef inside. They were really tasty, but one bite filled you up. It's unlikely this would be a dish your cardiologist would recommend. The advertised grits turned out to be cream of wheat; good cream of wheat, but cream of wheat nevertheless. The star of the breakfast show was the coffee, strong and flavorful with a boatload of chicory.

The storefronts were right out of a 1920s movie set. Facing a cobblestoned street complete with long lines of large flower baskets hanging above a lush green river bank, which leads to the pristine Cane River. The only thing this scene needed was a large bulldozer to remove all the modern cars parked on Front Street, and replace them with proper vintage classic cars. Phil and I could provide those at a very reasonable price, but I digress.

> Always leave early enough to catch the sunrise.

I love hardware stores, and the one we wandered into was from the past—a very upscale past. The shelves were made of real wood. There was a large table displaying nothing but multicolored marbles like the kind we played with as kids. There were nuts and bolts and pipes, car water pump belts and about anything else you can think of, but it's all displayed the way it was in earlier days. The cash register was mechanical, and about the size of a mini-refrigerator. No one was in a hurry, just like the good ole' days!

Reluctantly, we mounted our mechanical steeds the next morning and pointed them West to return to our time.

Our very first gas stop reminded us that we were in East Texas and had left the movie set. We ventured into a small inconvenience store, also a gas station, for a comfort break when Phil noticed a sign on the women's restroom that read: *No men allowed in women's restroom.*

Trying to lighten things up a bit, he sauntered over to the register and mentioned to the bear in women's clothing that he wanted to file a discrimination complaint. He went on to share that there was a sign on the women's restroom warning men not to enter, but there was no such sign on the men's restroom excluding women. The bear lost it. She glared at Phil and snarled, "Well if you go in there and expose yourself to my daughter, the police will be the least of your worries." This was clearly not what Phil expected. I did try to lift his spirits by telling him he did have that look, you know, a little like a pervert. This seemed to make him feel better. We hit the road pretty fast after that.

We had planned to take the same route back, but we couldn't remember the exact turns we had missed along the way to Natchitoches. The scenery heading back West was just as lovely, even though we missed different turns on the way home.

The second gas stop left us cornered by two locals who claimed to have ridden their Harley to Canada. The very petite man cornered Phil and was talking nonstop. His lady friend, who was about the size of a U-Haul trailer, followed me around talking about their motorcycle adventures. She said she took her pet squirrel with them on all their trips, keeping the squirrel between her breasts so it would stay warm. She admitted that sometimes she had to raise her arms so a cool breeze could come in through her armpits and the squirrel could get some air. I reported her to PETA shortly after. Poor squirrel.

Back on the road, we made our afternoon beer stop in Hearn, Texas. We drank a few beers and had taco salad. Our waitress was attentive until a young police officer came in and cornered the attractive young lady in the kitchen, right when I needed the check. I had to pour a bucket of cold water over the two to pry them apart. We managed to get out of there without being arrested. There must not be enough motels in this town.

Somewhere along the next stretch of road, Phil passed me and motioned to stop on a little dirt lane. Seems he had run the onboard diagnostics on his new Indian and an alert message popped up on screen: #428. He whipped out his phone and opened his Indian Diagnostics phone app. Phil actually has an app that works like a pocket mechanic. His phone revealed that the alert was related to his kickstand. It had dropped down an inch, and he needed to pull it back up. I found this amusing. I could be running 100 mph on my Harley, the kickstand could drop all the way down or fall off, and the Harley would not give a flying fish. Death by technology!

During the trip, we came up with a game of making *executive orders* we plan to enact when one of us is elected President:

1. No town with a population fewer than 15,000 are allowed to have speed limits lower than 45 mph.

2. Every town in America is required to have at least as many beer joints as churches.

3. Shopkeepers in small, redneck, West Texas towns should get free Xanex for daily consumption.

4. To minimize our carbon footprint, encourage motorcycle riding. Raise all gas prices 1¢ per gallon to fund a free gas program for all motorcycle riders.

We're still working on it.

Cars pulling out in front of you because they "do not see you" is a total MYTH. They do not give a shit. Consciously or unconsciously the auto driver is not threatened by a cycle because your are not a Mack truck or a Greyhound Bus. Motive does not make a rat's ass. Eventually a car is going to pull out in front of your ass and you best have a Plan B.

Save Gas, Get Off My Ass

A great way to improve your gas mileage and extend the life of your brake pads is to swear off tailgating. Everyone knows that pushing on the gas pedal uses gas. Any time you push the brake pedal, even the lightest tap, you have to use the gas pedal to recover to your previous speed. Both pedals increase your carbon footprint.

So what does this have to do with tailgating? There is a natural ebb and flow to traffic, a moderate slowing followed by a return to the original speed. Tailgaters are constantly hitting their brakes. Courteous drivers leaving a respectable distance allow this space to close slightly when the person in front slows, which allows the distance to absorb the normal ebbs and flows of traffic. Their brake lights are not constantly coming on and going off like Christmas tree lights. They manage space between vehicles with only the gas pedal virtually all the time.

> Sometimes the fastest way to get there is to stop for the night.

Watch for it on the road. Watch for those cars with constantly blinking brake lights. They are causing more drilling, our unquenchable oil dependency, and increased environmental damage—plus, the occasional case of road rage.

If you are guilty of tailgating, for the sake of the planet, please get off my ass.

"How sweet, he's smiling. He must be dreaming about me."

Photo by Jasper

Little did I know that in 4 days after this happy departure shot, I would be cutting a sofa in two with this new BMW.

That Looks Like a Couch

My son and I had a great ride to Port A. The rain subsided just minutes before our departure; the sun came up, the flowers bloomed, and the birds were singing—well, if Jonathan had not fired up the Harley, we may could have heard the birds singing. It was a beautiful, fun, and relaxing trip. Just too good to be true!

Little did I know that in 4 days after this happy departure shot, I would be cutting a sofa in two with this new BMW.

Lots of time walking on the beach and sitting in the hot tub catching up. When Jonathan is with you, he is totally with you. When he leaves for other parts of the world . . . well, he is with whoever he is with. That is the nature of Jonathan. We were together for five days at Port A and our rides down there and back were perfect. I was on an RT1200 BMW and he took his favorite ride: my old 1993 Harley Police Bike.

Back in Austin, Jonathan and I said our good-byes, and I proceeded to take the BMW to the car wash about dusk. Given that we had been on the Gulf Coast for five days, a wash was mandatory. The wash job subsequently called for a quick ride to blow the water off.

A few of my ass-tro-logical safety planets were beginning to align, but damn the torpedoes. For one, it had gotten dark. Second, bazillions of working people were trying to escape the insanity of Austin and frantically trying to get to the insanity of their homes, via Ranch to Market Road 620. Last, I had been riding with Jonathan, and we did not go much over 80 mph. He was on the Harley and it seems like you are going fast on a Harley at 80. Not true with the BMW. I needed my speed fix. Logically, the water droplets from the car wash would blow off more efficiently at higher speeds. All the above translates into my having my head up my ass.

With the BMW wet but all clean, I quickly became the pace car (cycle) on RM 620 headed west. Lo and behold, there appeared out of the night a huge newly upholstered love seat sitting upright smack in the middle of the passing lane. Coincidentally, I was using the passing lane to pass a car that was in the turtle lane. The turtle was doing about 70 mph.

Well, any experienced biker knows one thing for certain. When on a collision path with an obstacle, be it sofa or moose, you can either swerve or brake. Doing both at the same time will drop the bike quickly with the low side hitting the pavement first, rider in tow. These situations leave little time for contemplation or committee meetings. Pick curtain A or curtain B, and damn fast or it will be, well, curtains.

I swerved right toward the car I was in the

process of passing. I hit the sofa solidly with the left-side rigid luggage compartment, ripping it off and sending it flying into the middle lane.

The laws of geometry and dynamics came into play, sending the bike in a direction away from the car I was passing but in the direction of the two lanes of oncoming traffic. Fortunately, there was a center turn lane available. I had that fourteen-foot change lane in which to straighten the bike out of a serious wobble. If I could do it, I would avoid a head-on collision with an SUV. Thankfully, I was going fast enough to pull it off without going down. Speed stabilizes a motorcycle. The bike won out in this pool game where the cycle and sofa were the balls and RM 620 was the pool table. The sofa lost. I got another motorcycle safety experience.

About the time I had made it to the side of the road to throw up a perfectly good hamburger, the cowboy came back after his newly upholstered but now destroyed sofa that had blown out of his pickup truck. Needless to say, we had a spirited chat, but that is another story.

Never do less than 40 miles before breakfast.

Riding in small groups is safer than riding alone. Your visibility goes up dramatically, and sooner or later one of you is going to need tools, repair advice, a support vehicle, or buddy that will tell you when you're too drunk to drive!

Photo by Nathan Gibson

I never saw a gas station in Bali though there must be one. Jonathan (pictured above) and I bought gas for the bikes from young children peddling petrol in used vodka bottles. The "stations" looked more like lemonade stands.

Bali, Indonesia, At Last

A s background, my son is a missionary in Indonesia. Every other generation in our family is very religious with the off generations being heathens and alcoholics. Did I dodge a bullet or what?

The chaos of getting through Indonesian customs, getting a visa, and finding the greeting area paid off with a big smile from Jonathan. After a long awaited and much relished hug, it felt as if I had been with him only yesterday. He looked good, thin but tan and healthy and smiling.

Jonathan immediately began to pull my leg, just like the good ole days. His first attempt was to tell me that in the interest of time, traffic flexibility and so forth, he had rented a motorbike for $3 to pick me up as opposed to a cab. I went along with it. I had been up thirty-four hours by this time and decided to just let him run with it. Keep in mind I had a full backpack to support my two-month-plus walkabout plus my small leather backpack that is with me all the time.

I felt a bit faint as I watched him select a worn-out 100cc Honda out of a pile of creatively parked similar vehicles. This was no joke! It had a nice seat for one small person without luggage. Unfortunately, it started, and the fun began!

Driving conditions weren't great. We had to drive on the left side of the road sometimes. There was very heavy traffic in the height of tourist season—with the bonus of a religious holiday (rama-dama-ding-dong or the like). We heard a copious use of horns. Most must have gotten stuck. Unannounced gonad-busting speed bumps littered the roads, alternating with potholes. Frequent "zebra walks," caused a lot of confusion because occasionally a westerner would actually try to stop at one of them and would be rear-ended as a reward. The average speed of a car is 5 mph. Motorcycles race around others on sidewalks at warp speed. Every vehicle was too close to the next, way too close.

> Four wheels move the body.
> Two wheels move the soul.

Jonathan has ridden with me in cars and on motorcycles all of his life, and no doubt I have scared him a time or two. In twenty-five minutes in the city of Bali, my son avenged twenty-five years, and he enjoyed it thoroughly.

En-route Conversation

Me (screaming)
"Jonathan, how many little piece-of-shit motos like this do they scrape off the road a day here?"

Jonathan laughs.

Me (screaming)
"Jonathan, is it against the law here to look back before you change lanes?"

Jonathan laughs.

Me (still screaming)
"My backpack is wider than your handlebars. If my straps catch a car's rearview mirrors, we are going to stop very suddenly right before we drop to the pavement!"

Jonathan laughs.

Me
"Holy shit, Jonathan!"

Jonathan laughs.

And so forth, until we arrived at Hotel Un. We were only three blocks away from a beautiful beach. I had a much-deserved large beer, and then we were off to watch the sunset over pristine Sanur beach!

The next day we planned to tour the island on motorcycles. If you can call them motorcycles. The best ones were scrap heap quality by U.S. standards. The largest ones were 125cc and did not have enough power to pull a sick boy off the potty…but that is what was available. On the upside they were $3 per day. I asked Jonathan if we were going to a motorcycle shop to rent bikes. He got a laugh out of that. He explained that the process was that he would mention to a hotel employee[3] that we wanted two motos at 9 a.m. the following morning. I asked if we paid in advance and needed to sign any insurance or other documents. He laughed out loud at this ridiculous question. He explained that no money was exchanged until we showed back up, whenever that was. He also said there was no paperwork and no insurance. I had to asked another comical question.

"Well, what if something happens to the bike, a wreck or it gets stolen?" His response was not comical, at least not to me, he said, "they will kill you!" He said they know where

---

3   Jonathan had been in Indonesian 5 years by this time. He was fluent and knew the lay of the land.

you are all the time as they have friends and family who know the bikes and are accustomed to keeping up with white boys.

We were off the next day for a self guided tour of ancient Bali which is predominately Hindu. There is no shortage of temples and flower gardens and water features with lily ponds and ornate temple towers and statues. Every stop was either free or cost the equivalent of a dime U.S. It was culture shock but very good culture shock.

The destination, if there was one, was a Hindu holy ground overlooking a magnificent beach. We had shorts on so we were provided little blue skirts to cover our legs as we were on holy ground. Remarkably, the place was infested with spider monkeys, which are ranked right up there behind cows in terms of being sacred with the Hindus.

They were really cool to watch but they definitely had an agenda. Here is the scam. The monkeys would swoop down on your shoulders and grab your glasses or something out of your shirt pocket, then bound to the nearest tree.

The only way to get your stuff back was to buy some peanuts from the "very available" vendor. Obviously, the vendor had trained the monkeys to steal your stuff. He then could sell you peanuts. The vendor gets your money, the monkey gets peanuts and you get the green weenie!

The ocean views were breathtaking and the people and monkey watching were worth the price of admission which at equivalent of 25 cents (plus peanut payoffs) was pretty expensive for Bali.

Afterwards, Jonathan and I rode as close to the beach as we could get for a walk down the steep path to the ocean. We paid a local to watch the bikes. This kind of spooked me as I figured he would be the most likely one to steal them. Jonathan had been there before a number of times and knew who to trust. After a nice swim and hanging out on the beach we found the bikes right where we left them to my relief. By nightfall we had the bikes back to the rightful owners without incident.

Bali turned out to be one of the most beautiful,

least expensive and interesting places I had ever been. The beaches are deep and clean. Clean rooms off the ocean a few blocks start at about $20 a night but if you are willing to walk 7 or 8 blocks the same room is about $10. Beach front goes to U.S. prices.

Street crime there is relatively low there by third world standards. The Hindus are peaceful people. Having said that, Bali is a target for radical Islam. There have been 18 random bombings since 2000. So, once you get passed the possibility of getting blown up, Bali is really pretty safe.

I am going back there next month to visit Bali but also to ride the beautiful jungle forest of Bali's sister island, Flores, Indonesia.

There are four elements that impact a ride: the rider, the mechanical condition of the bike, the other guy, and road conditions. You may only have direct control of 2 out of 4 but *you* are the one responsible for all four. You are responsible for being on top of the situation and having a contingency plan for any combination of events.

If you think that the danger of riding is only about "the other guy," you should not be on two wheels.

Holy Sheep

N ew Zealand is lush—shades and hues of green unlike any I have ever witnessed, with the possible exception of Ireland.

The two islands, one about as far above the equator as the other is below, have many parallels. However, New Zealand is conspicuously more prosperous. I have decided it is because they are "Deeper in Sheep!"

There are zillions of sheep here. The soil is rich; moisture is plentiful and the grass is so thick that one acre here can, and does, support a hundred sheep. By contrast, one acre of Texas Hill Country can support one starving goat.

The picturesque pastures go for miles and miles and miles. But you do not see green pasture. Instead, you see overgrown white fluff balls bumping against one another. Imagine a couple thousand Johnson & Johnson cotton balls randomly thrown out on a regulation pool table. In either case, one can hardly see the green.

> They say life begins at 30, but it doesn't get real interesting until about 80 miles-per-hour.

On the ride this morning down the coastline, I had magnificent ocean views off to my left. More noteworthy—to my right—was what I did not see. I did not see condos, development, or 10,000-square-foot pretentious mansions. I did not see hotels or ocean-view restaurants. I saw sheep . . . mile after mile of sheep. I saw a Sheep Load of sheep. Their view from the mountainside must have been even better than mine. I do not know how they could look down to munch the grass with such breathtaking views.

Further, there do not seem to be any black sheep here. In Ireland, England, and Scotland, I noticed at least one black sheep in twenty— still a much better ratio than found in my own family. But that is another story. No Black Sheep. There are no black sheep in N.Z.

Finally, I think being born a sheep here in New Zealand is not such a baaaad deal, even if you discount the great views. If you were born a horse, someone would always be on your back; a cow, someone would be trying to milk you for all you are worth—but a sheep, all you have to do is grow hair. How hard can that be? It would be like being born into the Royal Family.

A sheep's only problem might be one of aging. Does a sheep's wool turn grey with age or is it like a female's hair in Texas that turns blond in the later years?

My shoes looked a little funky, but I have done dumber things.

It's Not Cool, Mate

A fter 10 hours on the bike I am having a glass of New Zealand merlot at a sidewalk café overlooking the Duneden downtown plaza. Centuries old cathedrals and townhalls guarding the quadrangle would put you to mind of Oxford, England except that it is December and the weather is brilliant. The plaza is a park of two rows of beautiful old Elm trees, pregnant with spring green leaves, leading to a giant Christmas tree, heavy with decoration and lights. A very strange thing for a person accustomed to the northern hemisphere, strange but acceptable.

The day did not start out this way. Forecasts were gloom and doom. The night before, which was my last night in Tararu I asked a local bloke about the prospect of heavy weather given the forecasts.

He responded, "Well I'll tell ye mate, what ye gotta do is ye go ta bed, ya see, then ya wake up tomorrow morning, mate…then you'll know won't ya?"

I told him words could not express how much help he had been.

Next morning, i.e. this morning, it was raining. Blowing sideways, it was very cold for a bike ride into the mountains. My trip plan was for one of my longer days into one of the higher altitudes to Mount Cook and the loop of snow covered peaks surrounding it. My bags were light as I was wearing every piece of clothing I had brought with me.

I had rain gear but no boots, only my water resistant walking shoes. Knowing that my feet getting wet in these temperatures was not a good option, I proceeded to cover my shoes with the plastic trash bags out of the motel room and duct taped them to conform to my shoes.

I shuffled up to the motel office to check out. A 40-ish couple who happened to be bikers owned the place and the boot arrangement amused, shocked and appalled them.

John brought out his cycle boots and insisted that I wear them to the other side of the island and return them in several days to a cousin of his who lived in a town I would be passing thru. When I resisted, he made a compelling argument that the bags could get tangled in the gearshift or worse yet the break, could be dangerous.

When that argument failed, he was exasperated and exclaimed, "It is just not cool mate, you are on a beautiful bike and have bags over ya feet, it's just not cool!"

Why can I not convince people that some of us think it is cool not to be cool?

I was off into the rain, creative foot apparel and all with the rain coming down torrentially and a big smile on my face. I was not being cool!

The weather was a bit tough for a few hours but got better by noon and turned out to be a splendid riding day. The wild flowers and snow-covered mountains were stunning. Riding beside endless lakes that were as blue as the waters of the Caribbean. Not being cool just made my day.

Most "bike drops," which are always embarrassing, happen when parking on sloped terrain, a soft surface, or when you are watching some hot young lady walk by in spandex shorts. Don't do those things at the same time. Together or independently, all of these things can get your chrome scuffed up.

Sailing Through Mexico

W hy sailing?

Powerboats go straight from point A to point B. Sailboats jibe and tack, rarely pointing toward their desired destination. Sailboat people have patience and tend to be detail oriented. The mantra of a sailboat person is "nowhere in parcticular to go and all the time in the world to get there."

I am a powerboat person. I am not a patient or detailed person. I have friends who are patient and detail oriented; all of them are also gifted in judgment. All of them elected not to accompany me on a 1,385-mile meandering motorcycle trip through Mexico to beautiful Acapulco.

After standing in lines at multiple visa, cycle insurance, registration, and other bureaucratic windows at the Tamaulipas depot on the Mexican border crossing at Reynosa, I was sailing on my own. Rarely was I going in the direction of my friend's home in Oaxtepec, but rather sailing in that general direction. Much of the time it looked as if I was lost, perhaps because I was, in fact, quite lost. In the morning I kept the sun to my left, my face in the wind, and made damn sure Mexico City stayed safely eastward. I did not need to tangle with Mexico City after nightfall.

Keep your bike maintained. Motorcycle boots are NOT comfortable for walking.

Day One

The grand plan was to make it to Oaxtepec by dark. I had a friend there on a temporary engineering assignment. The distance was under seven hundred miles, and I have pushed my old police bike through a number of thousand-mile days before. It looked like a piece of cake ...*on the map.*

Within a few hours, a major road deviation in San Javier sent me thirty miles off course onto a dirt "pig's path." Prior to the deviation, I thought I was already on a "pig's path." This road set a new standard for "pig's paths," even for rural Mexico. Traffic, all on the detour route, was mostly large trucks and buses. The dust was indescribable. Visibility was ten feet max. I learned that it was impossible to keep a sane distance from the vehicle in front of me. Regardless of speed, road surface, or driving conditions, any distance allowed was seen by the driver behind me as an open invitation to move up in the queue. With a bandana around my nose, my dirty goggles on my face, and a death grip on my handle grips, I hung in with this ragtag desert caravan.

The rule of the road seemed to favor vehicle size and driver courage. The trucks were more forgiving of road splitting, the process of motorcycles advancing between vehicles by taking advantage of their more compact size. The buses took a different attitude. I found bus drivers, especially near Toluca, anxious to compress my bike into something smaller. My asshole was what they seemed to have in mind.

While more friendly, or at least less hostile, the trucks frequently had loads threatening to come off. In the case of the gravel trucks and sugar cane trucks, some of the load did come off. A steady stream of fine gravel or an occasional sugar cane spear coming at you is the perfect fix for a person with a mild addiction to an adrenaline rush. Pancho, a friend familiar with cycling in Mexico, had warned of the sugar canes, but I thought he was just adding a bit of color. Pancho knows his sugar cane!

The deviation cost me three hours, but I eventually made it to San Juan del Rio, where I missed a turn and ended up in the town center. It was here that I learned that the petrol attendants would agree with you on any direction you point to as a direction to any town you choose. Perhaps they did not know and were unwilling to admit ignorance of the direction of the nearest large town. Perhaps they did not give a damn. Most likely, they figured that if you did not know where you wanted to go, any road would get you there. I also learned that truck drivers stopped for a break at one of the roadside stands are a good resource for directions. I found them very willing to draw a map.

The chances of making it to Maxie's place by nightfall were growing slim.

Toluca
...a long time later, still same day

If I never go there again, it will be too soon. Throughout Mexico signs to prominent cities pointing left do not necessarily mean to turn left. Such a sign could mean to make a U-turn, a *retorno*. This means you are going in the wrong direction on the right road. The same city is rarely referenced in these signs twice in sequence. The same road is marked by randomly selected cities on that route. Road numbers, while abundant on the map, are nonexistent on directional signs, and designation of *norte*, *sur*, *este*, or *oeste* would be far too much to expect.

My Harley will burn a spark plug if you choke it the slightest bit too long. High elevations have the same effect as choking. The air is thinner and, therefore, the gas is richer . . . same as choking. Upon starting the engine that morning in Jalpan, I found my baby ran more like a dog than normal, so I knew the plugs were on their last leg. Not a problem, as I had asked the Harley dealership to drop a spare set of plugs under the seat in preparation for this trip. After about two hours of "sailing" around Toluca, I was down to one cylinder. It was time to change the plugs. I was in a very rough section of town. Fortunately, this area was identical to the balance of Toluca, so location was irrelevant.

I pulled up on the sidewalk to avoid death while changing the plugs, only to be joined by two policía. They rode a couple of off-road Yamahas that looked like they had 500,000 rough miles apiece on them. The bikes may have been 250cc, but likely were smaller. I proceeded to change the plugs, only to be horrified to find that the Harley dealership had packed plugs for a Sportster. They almost fell into the cylinder when I tried to install them. I scraped and cleaned the old plugs as my new uniformed and very armed friends looked on. One policeman even recleaned a plug for me! I read this as a good sign until I pondered that, if he planned to end up with the bike, he needed it to run.

The bike ran well after the plugs were reinstalled, so I pointed to my map and communicated the next town on my list of towns. It was the point of my next major turn and was eighteen miles south of Toluca. They flailed their hands and arms, both speaking Spanish to me at once. The language really wasn't much of a barrier given that I can't hear anyway. The sun was falling. Having been on the road for twelve hours, I was exhausted, frustrated, and pretty much exasperated. Using my broken Spanish and a phrase book, the map, and two crisp hundred-peso notes, I communicated a deal that would have them leading me to the desired turn off at Tenango de Arista for the two hundred pesos. Bingo! The language barrier crumbled under the weight of free enterprise and was replaced by instant smiles and international understanding.

With their blue lights flashing and their Yamahas buzzing at about twice the posted speed limit, I was escorted, unencumbered, through red lights and stop signs for eighteen miles. For the equilvant of $20 U.S., I was El Presidente for forty-five minutes. It did occur to me that we might be headed to a quiet place to parcticipate in a redistribution of wealth, or perhaps worse, but at that point I had few choices. They got me to my road and were happy with the deal. Me too! The setting sun remained to my right so I was headed south—a good sign.

On to Oaxtepec, I could still make it! Within twenty minutes of being El Presidente—the height of my roller coaster ride of emotions that day—I plunged back into desperation. I was on a toll road and came very fast upon a split in the road. Both options were signed with cities on my list. I did not realize that I had already gone through one, so it was one of those retorno tricks. Too late—I was on a limited access road going north, the wrong direction. I pulled over and checked the map. Damn it! I was not going back to Toluca! While there was not an access road, there was a mud road adjacent to the toll road leading to a village of cardboard-box huts.

A barrier of earth about five times the size of a speed bump and of similar shape separated me from the northbound toll road. I was about a quarter mile north of the retorno I needed to take to continue on the southbound toll road. I negotiated the dirt road toward the dingy village of dilapidated houses to within a few hundred yards of the retorno, where the dirt road veered left. I had a decision to make. Was I going to try to jump the giant Hump and then go against one-way traffic for a few hundred yards, or was I going to do the sensible thing and go north in search of another retorno?

It was at this point that two little figures appeared on my shoulders. One was Pancho arguing reason. He said, "You dumb-ass, you have not stopped for a break nor eaten anything since breakfast fourteen hours ago. *Go North.* Find a hotel. Finish the trip tomorrow." Upon my other shoulder was the figure of my late dad, God rest his soul. He said, "Go for it, you whimp! Rest is for weenies! You told Maxie you would be there *today*. A man is only as good as his word! Plenty of time for rest after the grave!"

I got off the bike and looked carefully at the Hump separating me from my destination. If I hit it at an angle, the Harley would go over it. If I hit it too fast, I would be unable to stop before sliding into 80 mph northbound traffic. There was no emergency lane, just two fast lanes. The shoulder was eighteen inches at best, then the Hump. If I hit it too slow, the Harley would straddle the Hump like a seesaw, and I'd be stuck for the duration. I had this vision of how pissed my mom would be if I did something requiring her to have to travel here to erect one of those little white crosses. And after that, who would water the plastic flowers?

I decided to go for it. I erred on the side of safety and hung the Harley, teeter-tottering on the mound of dirt and rocks. I tried rocking back and giving it gas. This brilliant idea only served to dig the rear wheel in up to the axle. I got off the bike. It was perfectly stable, no kickstand required. The frame was solidly on the ground with the rear wheel buried in the earth. Holy shit! The sun was setting and five hombres had come out of Hut-City to observe from about twenty-five yards. They had their arms folded and had the look of vultures watching a roadkill varmint taking its last few kicks before jumping into action.

Fortunately, I had done something around the same level of stupid years ago and so had a recovery plan. If this ever happens to you, lay the bike completely on its side and rotate it like a clock hand 90 degrees. This aligns the bike with the ridge of the hump and moves the wheel out of its hole. Lift the bike back upright. Fire the engine up, wait for an opening in the oncoming traffic, and then open the throttle and go for the *retorno* with abandon! Bueno, I was heading south again!

I could still make it that night if everything went perfectly. I hit Santa Maria, which signified that I was headed due east toward Oaxtepec. Magnifico! I was so excited that I failed to see the Mother of all Speed Bumps. I hit it so hard that my Harley left the ground for the first time in its life. I barely maintained control of the bike! Looking left, I saw four policía watching in amazement. I was not concerned in the least bit.

Factoid: Severe pain in the groin area, from

harsh contact with the gas tank, trumps all concerns about the *policía*.

I slowed to 15 mph and limped out of town, having provided the local policía with more than a moderate amount of amusement.

It did not take long to get lost again. I can't really blame it on the signs. I was tired and making bad decisions. After I passed the same (relatively nice) hotel twice, I made a deal with myself that I would call it a day after one more disaster.

This did not take too long to occur. The next small town was the scene of a political rally, and traffic was backed up for as far as I could see. I had made it into the town center before comprehending the hopelessness of the situation. I took a left to try to return to the aforementioned hotel. Amazingly, no one else was using that road! Near the end of the road, I discovered the reason: the rupture of a waterline had the dirt street covered in what I thought was just a few inches of water. With enough speed, I could splash right through! You got it; I got her stuck up to the axles—this time both of them. I was covered in mud and looked and felt like a real asshole. Asshole or no, two of the locals were happy to push me out for fifty pesos each. I worked my way backward to the aforementioned hotel slinging bits of mud and water along the way.

From the hotel, I called my friend and advised him I was having too many photo opportunities and too much fun chatting with the people along the way, and besides, I wanted to spend the night so as not to rush the trip. He and I have traveled together before so he knew that this was total bull shit.

After a well-deserved hot shower, I had chips and salsa, a nice steak, and six Coronas for under $13 U.S. I was on the El Presidente apex of my emotional roller coaster again. Suddenly, this trip was not a stupid, impetuous idea but a great adventure!

Day Two

Totally contrary to the straight east-to-west road on the map, the road from Tenango de Arista to Oaxtepec goes over two mountain ranges and is not "due" any direction. Further, it goes through many little towns where the main road goes straight but the correct road with a "delayed directional sign" requires a turn. A "delayed directional sign" is one that is marked correctly about two hundred yards after your turn. This assumes you made the correct turn—effectively, no signage if you happened not to be clairvoyant.

A few unplanned sightseeing adventures later, I made it to Oaxtepec and proceeded to my friend's address. Totally consistent with the trip to date, his home address was the identical address for two houses on the same street about half a mile apart. Of course, I found the wrong one. Ultimately, I arrived, having created a 1,100-mile, two-day trip out of a 700-mile, one-day trip, but I was there!

The road to Acapulco was magnificent and a perfect ride for a cycle. The toll ride down was expensive and little better than the free road, which I took on the return trip. Both had adequate petrol. While in Acapulco, I chartered a $100-per-day boat and managed to catch two marlins, both over 150 pounds. Life is good; the trip was (again) a stroke of genius!

The Harley did fine except that the gears started feeling a bit clunky as I neared Mexico City while I headed back home. I was hoping that I was imagining things. Unfortunately, I was not. A decision had to be made. Find a Harley shop in Mexico City or take a chance that the failing synchronizers would not get me back to the States. I had brought an extra clutch cable, but damn, I forgot to bring an extra transmission! You guessed it; I decided to go for it.

North through Mexico City looked incredibly easy. Just take the autopista (ring road) north. I soon learned that motos are banned from the autopista as a result of bandits using fast bikes on this road to take advantage of stopped traffic. The banditos were robbing and often shooting car drivers in the head, then using the speed and flexibility of the cycle to disappear.

The alternative was to go straight through the city, stoplight by stoplight. I have never had to protect my lane so aggressively. I am not a timid driver, but this was a whole new league. World-class "chaos and aggression" comes to mind. A group of banditos on custom cycles fell in behind and beside me for a few miles, disappeared, and then reappeared behind me. I figured they went away to smoke a joint and caucus. Thankfully, they decided that I was not worth the trouble. After a while, they disappeared again for good. Mexico City took its toll on the weak clutch. At the right RPMs all but fourth gear worked okay, but downshifting took both the right RPMs and a lot of pressure. Unlike my Harley friends around the world, I was revving the engine for a legitimate purpose. I was trying to get my baby to take a gear!

I stopped for only fuel and military road checks. The cycle was popular at the checks and my paperwork was checked over a dozen times. I was told at one that I had a lot of baggage and the check would take a very long time. A fifty-peso note shortened this to a few seconds. This bribe was probably avoidable, but I was unarmed.

Most of the time the militia and the policía were friendly, though I could have gotten by with fewer of them. There is something about a nervous seventeen-year-old kid in a uniform with an AK-47 that makes me anxious. Actually, the practice of open grazing of donkeys, horses, and cattle along and in between the roads poses a greater danger than the law or the crime factor. The possibility of mechanical failure in a desolate or unsafe area comes in a close second.

I made the trip back in two days, stopping only in Matehuala for a dinner, a night's rest, and a breakfast. As usual, I had to push my bike into the room with me to avoid a change in ownership. The transmission got worse, but I made it almost to Austin before the last incident of the trip.

I ran into heavy weather (tornados spawned by Katrina, I learned later) as I approached Austin. I thought it was a little cloud, and after what I had driven through, I was not about to stop for a few drops of rain. Adding to the challenge, and after twelve hours on the road, I forgot to replace my gas cap after a fill-up between San Antonio and Austin. I smelled gas, which was splashing in abundance over a hot engine and exhaust pipes. The driving rain, wind, and walls of water blowing off the wheels of semis were demanding my full attention. Now I was trying to drive with one hand over the gas tank fill hole. After fifteen minutes and a few near misses on IH 35, I decided to stop and buy a roll of aluminum foil. I made a massive ball of the foil and screwed it down into the tank, allowing it to take the shape of a gas cap. This was not pretty, but it got me to Austin.

In summary, Mexico was great fun and a memorable ride. Taking the trip alone and with limited Spanish demonstrated suspect judgment. Taking it on a ten-year-old bike with 131,000 miles on it also demonstrated suspect judgment. I figure the two cancel each other out, so it was probably one of those good ideas that I will probably not follow through on again any time soon.

Protective gear is a touchy subject. Some say leather is expensive and that skin will grow back. Others are decked out like Hollywood stunt riders. It is a personal choice, but wearing *no* protective gear clearly adds risk. According to studies done by the NHTSA, you are 40% more likely to die in the event of an accident if you are not wearing a helmet.

**"I need a really loud horn.
My brakes are a bit spongey."**

Don't Go There: Antigua, Guatamala

Periodically, I get a bug to go to a Central or South American country to study Spanish and just hang out for a month or so. Invariably, I rent a moto and check out the countryside. Some folks take tour buses. Then again, some folks drive Volvo station wagons while others ride motorcycles. Some folks watch TV while others venture out into the world and have adventures. Some of us think that if you aren't living on the edge, you're taking up too much space.

The search for the moto rental place in Antigua, Guatemala, took way too much time. The city is not that big, unless you're walking. Using my broken Spanish, I asked the nice old señora who served me breakfast if she knew where to rent a moto. I followed her directions, walking across the city and half a mile into the countryside before I arrived at a place that only rented horses. Perhaps my Spanish is even worse than I think.

I trekked back into the city and located a scary place with a half-dozen dirty, dilapidated bikes out front. There was a hand-scribbled for rent sign in the door. It was a very poorly lit shop with moto parts strewn all over the greasy floor and on wobbly wooden shelves. I called out but got no answer. In the back of the large front room was a small, dingy office with a single exposed light bulb hanging over a desk. Behind the desk was a very drugged-out, disheveled American. His head was on the desk. He was totally out of it. I must have made a noise because just then, he looked up shakily with bloodshot eyes and mumbled, "What do you want?" I got the hell out of there. I wanted to rent a bike but not that badly.

The second place was better, kind of. It was a moto/auto dealership that also rented bikes. The bikes and cars were Hondas. They sold 750cc bikes and cars with engines not much larger. To be able to rent a bike over 150cc in a Third World country is about as good as it gets. I was excited. Then he explained the rental deposit.

In order to rent the bike, I had to allow him to run $7,000 on my credit card, which he would reverse when I brought the bike back. The bikes were nice by the standards of the area, but I can buy similar bikes for $3,000 all day long in the States. I had no choice; I let him run the card.

I know the scam, as it is common in Central America. The game is to get a large up-front deposit. Then they have an "associate" steal the bike from you. They keep your deposit, and "sell" the bike to the next customer when you are safely back in the States. Needless to say, you have to keep an eye on the bike. Know that you are being followed.

The second drawback is that you have to

sign something that says you will not go off the main roads into the most beautiful parts of the countryside. You are told that there are banditos and that those areas are lawless.

I had done some research on that topic the previous night. After enjoying more than a few beers with some Americans who had also rented bikes, I found out they had ventured into those forbidden areas. Banditos did, in fact, block the road to rob them. The American riding in the rear had managed to turn his bike around and scramble back to the nearest village, which had a one-man police department.

He was flailing his arms, explaining the robbery in progress when the cop calmly told him there was no way he was going up into the mountains, "There are banditos up there. It's dangerous."

Shortly thereafter, the American's friends came riding up. The banditos had only taken their money, did them no harm, and didn't take their motorbikes. So, as it turns out, it's not dangerous as long as you don't take very much money with you. Armed with that research, I rented my moto and headed to the forbidden, beautiful, mountainous, roads around Lake Atitlán.

Lake Atitlán is of unknown depth, being the crater left from a volcanic eruption in prehistoric times. Nestled between volcanoes and surrounded by small villages, the paths around the lake served up yet another wonderful cycling experience.

Saturday is not a holiday for the typical Guatemalan. It was difficult to suppress a twinge of guilt. I was sporting around on a moto, for which I paid a day's rent equal to a local's monthly income. I cruised by families including members across the generations, from small children to very old grandmas and grandpas, all toiling in the fields under a very hot sun.

By totally random chance, I had born in a different country, under different circumstances — circumstances that I have been arrogant enough to complain about at times. Regardless of the guilt I felt, it is important to note that these farmers did not seem unhappy, just poor, and extremely poor at that. Happiness, it seems, is all about expectations. Perhaps they should be concerned about me.

I stopped in at a roadside nursery/café. All the food was grown by the owner/cook, including the chickens running around in the yard. I grabbed an outside table very close to my rental bike and settled in for a wonderful meal. While waiting, I watched some of the largest hummingbirds I have ever seen feast on flowers growing in the hanging baskets.

The sun was starting to dip, and I had to get back to the city before dark. I was a little uneasy about meeting banditos after dark but much more concerned about the narrow dirt roads winding around the volcanic mountainside with drop-offs to forever. Guardrails are unheard of in this part of the world. Living on the edge is a way of life, but falling off the edge would be of suspect judgment.

By 7 p.m. I had turned my bike back in, got my deposit back, and was sipping on a quart of Gallo beer just half a block from my Homestay. Just another day in paradise!

Like I was saying... Protective gear is not just about helmets, boots, leather, and gloves. Reflective clothing can make a big difference in your visibility at dawn, dusk and night. It might be worth not being cool. Motorcycle cops have coined the term "high conspicability". The more conspicuous you are the better.

Photo by passerby

*That's me, pushing my bike down Lykavittos Hill
in Athens, Greece.*

When In Greece

There's the easy way, the difficult way, and the Greek way. And I learned this the Greek way. My needs were simple: I wanted to tour Athens on a motorcycle. I knew the density and craziness of car and cycle traffic would be worse than I had experienced in Rome. For those of us who have a mild addiction to adrenaline, danger is a good thing.

Getting directions in the world's oldest civilization is uncivil, so it took me half a day of walking in circles to find the bike rental shop. I have learned never to set my expectations too high on the quality of rental bikes, but these set a new high in low. The bike offered was a ten-year-old 150cc Asian bike with untold mileage and an untold number of drops. The paperwork necessary to get this piece of shit was extensive, but I endured the process and rode out, only to find there were no brakes. None. I eased around the block with only a few near misses, returning to the shop to demand a better cycle.

The owner, whom I would soon get to know better, was terribly apologetic and said, in very broken English, "I get you a gooood one. My beeest one because you are my friend!"

He did come back with a bike that had spongy, but existent, brakes. I left uneasy but happy.

There are twenty times the number of motorbikes in Athens than cars, so the cars just move along at a slow pace and the motorcycles swarm around them. Very much like small fish in the ocean swarm around slower, larger fish. If there are any traffic rules in Athens, I never figured them out. There were signs, but they were all in Greek, which is Greek to me.

My goal was to get to the summit of

Lykavittos Hill for very good views of Athens. I made it to the hill, but just as I got to the top, I felt something squishy. Squishy, as in, my back tire was flat. I didn't fret—I just did what guys do when they have a problem. I went into the little bar on the summit and had a beer or two.

There I presented my rental agreement to the main bartender and asked him to call the moto rental place. I instructed him to give the shop owner the following options:

1. come out and fix my flat tire
2. bring me another bike
3. or, allow me to leave the bike at the restaurant while I get a cab to my hotel

After some debate and much flailing of arms, the waiter told me that I needed to talk to the moto rental owner myself. He brought me the phone, and the owner and I launched into a discussion that went something like this:

Owner
"I know you have a big-a-problem, but it is a U-problem!"

212 MOTORCYCLE MISADVENTURES

Me
"What exactly do you mean by that?"

Owner
"You have a flat. So you fix it."

Me
"I did not rent this %$^@* bike
to work on. I rented it to drive!"

Owner
"U-Fix it."

Me
"Listen, Asshole, I am at the top of a
mountain. I can leave this piece of shit here
and take a cab, you can come get it and bring
me another bike, or I can very simply push this
bike off the side of the mountain."

Silence on the other end of the line, and then
"I have-a-U passport."

Rules are different in different parts of the
world. To get a bike in Athens, you have to
surrender your passport. So he had me by the
short hairs.

I just hung up and wandered out into the parking lot totally pissed off. There was another moto guy parked there who told me that about two miles down the hill there was a motorcycle shop that would fix the tire. I pushed the bike down the hill, waited a couple of hours for the tire repair, and was on my way again. I headed out around dusk. The traffic was furious and I was a bit tense, so I flipped on my headlights— only to discover the lights didn't work. I had no lights, dusk was quickly turning into dark, and I was twenty miles from my hotel.

Holy shit!

I was too afraid to drive on crazy Athens streets at night with no lights, so I drove on the sidewalks, to the surprise of a lot of pedestrians. It took a while, but I did make it back to my hotel alive. The next day I drove the bike another couple of miles back to its rightful owner, gave him some B.I.F. (Blunt Immediate Feedback), and vowed to never rent a motorcycle in Athens again!

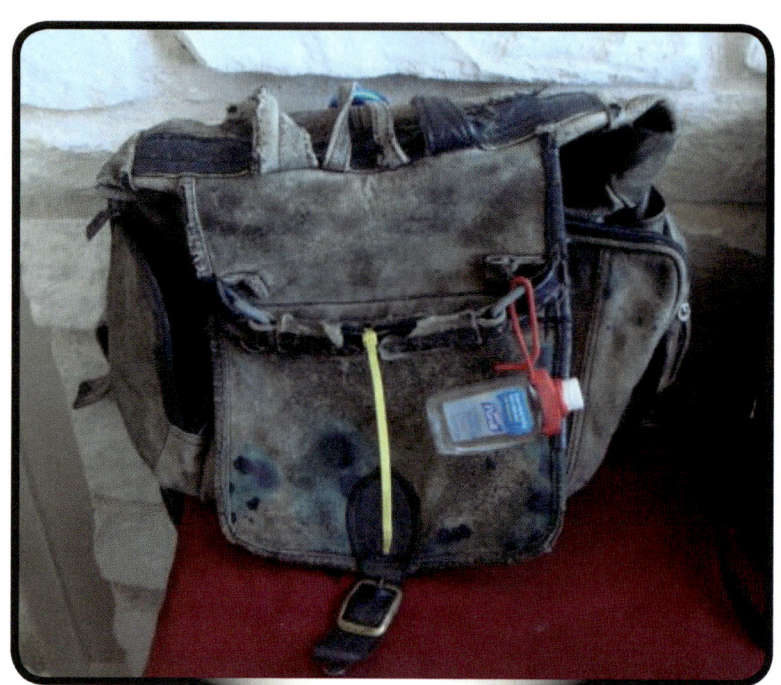

Photo by Nathan Gibson

This may look like a tattered black bag but it is my right arm. It hides my passport, travel tickets, credit cards, my phone, my laptop, my reading and sun glasses, my wallet and a stash of $100 dollar bills and has been around the world a couple of times.

Missing Black Bag

S unday shaped up to be a perfect ride day. I rolled the Harley out of its hiding place to check the tire pressure, oil, and fuel. Then I looked for any parts that were about to fall off. Each biker develops their own system for keeping up with their stuff. I use a black tank bag that is attached to my gas tank with magnetic flaps. It has a map window and enough room for a pair of reading glasses, wallet, phone, sunglasses, sunscreen, and more.

The old proverb goes like this: Don't put all your eggs in one basket. But my hero, Mark

Twain, said, "Put all your eggs in the one basket, and watch that basket." I took half of his advice. I knew exactly where I put all my eggs. You are about to hear about the basket!

After finishing the pre-flight checks, I shot off for the car wash for a quick spray down. I placed the bag against the wall just out of the splash zone. After the wash, I toweled off the bike and blasted out only to note that the tank bag was not riding on the tank. I had not made it but 2 miles down the road, so initially I wasn't worried. Not until I was rolling back toward the car wash stall could I see that the bag was not where I had left it.

Note: This bag had my life in it. That included my phone, wallet (containing several hundred dollars), driver's license, house and car keys— not to mention my two credit cards and only debit card.

In the stall where I had washed the Harley, there was now a very old Pontiac being washed by a young Latino gentleman. I dismounted, walked to within earshot, and said, "I left a black bag right here," pointing to the spot.

He replied, "No habla ingles."

Now, I had a high degree of certainty that my bag was in his car. I was also certain that the car was not going anywhere until I was proven wrong. I looked back at him and said, "Tengo bolso negra aquí. Yo llama la policía ahora, comprehenda?"

In case you are not bilingual, what I said roughly translates into "I have a black bag here. I call the police now, do you understand." Then, as if by some strange miracle, it seemed that my very bad Spanish caused him to remember his very good English.

He spoke up in the King's English, "Oh! Oh, that is your black bag?" then walked to his car and retrieved my bag from under the driver's seat. He handed it to me with a nervous smile on his face.

All's well that ends well: The contents of the bag were unmolested. I was off to a great ride having dodged another senior-moment (read "dumb ass" moment) bullet. In hindsight, I think the operative word in my little speech was policía.

Photos by Nathan Gibson

I took multiple shots of pavement, trying to catch a bike, traveling the length of a football field each second.

I had to push the button a full 3 seconds, or 900 feet, before the bike passed by just to get that red blur. No, I did not move the camera. A cycle at 200 mph is just a blur.

The Isle
Of Man

T he Isle of Man is a small charming island with 220 square miles of green pastures, stone fences that keep in the sheep, and a combination of cozy farming and fishing villages. This picturesque island, situated between Ireland and England, can best be described as sleepy. Except when it's not sleepy. Between the last few days of May and the first two weeks of June, it is not sleepy.

About 40,000 racing enthusiasts travel to this island of 86,000 inhabitants to witness the TT races. About 20,000 of them bring their motorcycles.

In 1904 the Auto-Cycle Club, organizers of a major motorcycle road race in England, got told to be gone with their dangerous event. The Isle of Man happily accepted the Tourist Trophy races and the rest is history. The first racing event was in 1905. The first 37.7-mile Snaefell Mountain Course race was run in 1911 and has continued every year since.

When my company asked me if I was interested in transferring to England, I could not wait to ship my motorcycle and hop on a plane with a small hand bag of personal items. To be within striking distance of the Isle of Man TT was icing on the cake!

The first time I attended the races was in 1998. We left South Fawley, Oxfordshire, about 9 a.m. in a driving rain[4] for the 200 mile trip to Liverpool where we had a 5 p.m. ticket on the ferry to Douglas, Isle of Man. Our motley crew consisted of English workmates Nigel, Colin, and Phil in addition to my 19 year old son, Jonathan, and myself. Nigel, Phil, and Colin were on Ducati's, I was riding my R1200S BMW, and Jonathan

---

4   If you do not ride your motorcycle in the rain while you are in England, you do not ride.

was on the 1993 Harley Police bike I had shipped from the States.

We were probably driving too fast for Jonathan's experience level, but he handled it well. Especially when his left handlebar grip came off! Driving 85 mph in high winds and heavy rain, he only had the right acceleration hand to manage that 650 lb. bike. But Jonathan did not lose his cool. He just eased off the gas, did not hit the brake, and veered to the left side of the road. One extra challenge for us was driving on the left. We wrapped a ton of electrician's tape on the handle bar, and forced the grip back on. In 20 minutes, we were back on the road (at a slower pace).

Bike traffic got progressively thicker as we approached the ferry, which was good, as it told us we were likely on the right road. Loading the ferry was a cluster to say the least. Ferries are set up for hauling cars not cycles. This ferry could accommodate about 500 cycles per trip. Our instructions were to park our bike very close to the bike we road in behind. Big burly guys then roped our bikes together. In the end, they built a very successful motorcycle spider web. The ferry has an enclosed upper deck and an open upper deck on top of that. Did I say deck? I should have said upper bars. Did I mention we had access to upper bars for the entire 5 hour trip? Unloading the ferry in Douglas, the largest town on the island, was cluster phase II with further alcohol enhancement. But it happened without incident that anyone noticed.

Douglas was fun. Bikes were ubiquitous. Bikers were aglow with happiness at being around so many like-minded souls and so many cycles to gawk at. Ages old Victorian hotels lined the streets in Douglas, but we did not go the posh route. We rented rooms from one of the many island residents who, for a price, open up their homes to the onslaught. We lucked out. Not because we are lucky but because we booked 6 months in advance. Our Homestay was on the racecourse with a balcony overlooking the road-racing street circuit. Yea!

Keep in mind that in 1998, everyone (which would include me) did not own a smart phone with video capabilities. We could see a turn from our balcony, but we were on a straight where speeds reached 195+ mph. The bikes were a blur and far too much for the shutter speed of my camera. I had a digital camera. The same one I once used to take hundreds of snaps of the pavement with no sign of a motorcycle.

It is very difficult to describe the speeds, in order of magnitude, that these motorcycles are reaching on this crooked 37.7-mile track. The winners average 130 mph while negotiating over 200 turns that wind through a couple of towns and a dozen small villages. The circuit is complete with narrow bridges, stone walls, and ancient buildings that hug the road on either side.

On the short straights, speeds routinely approach 200 mph. Bruce Anstey, a New Zealander, set the record of 206 mph on a Suzuki 1000cc machine. Those speeds on that treacherous track are only two of the reasons why the TT is perhaps the most dangerous race on earth. There were 5 fatalities at each of the two events I attended.

There have been a total of 265 fatalities in the TT's 110 years of existence. Eighteen of these were spectators and officials. This race is not for those adverse to risk.

Ships are safe in harbor but that is not what ships are for.

Numerous writers are given credit for that quote, though I am not one of them.

Photo by Nathan Gibson

Some of our days were long. I would come back from arranging a room and Jonathan would be asleep on the cycle.

Speaking of danger, Mad Sunday falls on the Sunday between the time trials and the races. You may know that mad in Brit-speak means crazy. Well, on Mad Sunday, all bikers who brought bikes are welcome to drive the circuit at whatever speed their courage allows.

I have ridden Mad Sunday twice. I did not allow my son to ride because it is Mad. The varied speeds and rider competencies add to the natural challenge of those crooked little trails through fairyland. It was normal to be passing an old vintage doing 65 when a crotch rocket would be passing you and a faster crotch rocket be passing that rider. All of these close encounters happen pretty much mirror to mirror due to the density of bike traffic. It is definitely an adrenaline rush.

The good news is that races are scheduled every other day. So, everyone could take a slower more sane tour of this island, stopping for pictures of windmills and fishing villages and what ever on the off days. I recall one incident when Jonathan, my 19-year-old son, rear-ended my BMW on one of those slower tours. We had pulled off to take some photos and needed to get back on the road in a blind curve. There was a lot of moto traffic so I emphasized to Jonathan that when I picked a time to break in, he was to nail it so as not to be hit. Well, I picked a time and started to make my break but almost immediately heard the familiar whine of an oncoming (but out of sight) crotch rocket. This gave me second thoughts. I stopped. Jonathan followed instructions and nailed it. Then my 10-year-old Harley rammed my new BMW. I was pushed to the edge of traffic but managed to avoid being hit. We got a story out of it. It was nothing the BMW folks back in England could not fix, and no one was hurt.

Other activities on the "off days" include various cycle club events, complete with music and food and tall tales of motorcycle adventures. I attended the Harley club event, which had a whopping 25 Harleys in attendance. Not exactly Sturgis! It was kind of nice to see the Triumphs, Ducatis, Nortons, BMWs, Vincents, Motoguzzis, Hondas, Yahamas, Suzukis, and Kawasakis dominate for a change.

The camaraderie of riding and being a spectator with my son and three friends made the trip what it was. We explored the island: A miniature Ireland complete with all the shades of green, friendly pubs, and good food.

Nigel and I attended the year before Jonathan

got to tag along. We can call it research. We suspected we might have a pint, so we left our cycles at the Homestay and walked the two miles into Douglas toward the craziness. It turned out to be a long night. Especially for Nigel.

Seems he and I got separated sometime around 2 a.m. Further, I was not real sure where our Homestay was, but I had the address. Cabs were totally booked full, so I ordered a pizza. I was not parcticularly hungry, but I slipped the driver an extra $10 to deliver the pizza and me to the Homestay. Nigel looked for me for far too long before walking home in the rain and ended up locked out of the house. While I was sleeping happily in my warm bed, Nigel slept on the concrete porch.

I cannot do justice to the races by describing them in words alone. If you have not experienced it yourself, I suggest you search YouTube for Isle of Man TT Race to see the live action. There is no substitute for the real thing, but a video of those bikes tearing past each other at 200 mph shows you exactly how close the riders are to each other and the stone walls. Those bridges and small hills I mentioned will send your front wheel up for what seems longer than physics should allow. If you are not a biker, you would still enjoy the Isle of Man. If you are a biker, you just must go! Put it on your bucket list.

You do not get old and stop riding. You stop riding and get old.

Animals happen. They happen more frequently at daybreak and dusk. If you are driving through an area where every truck you meet has a monster cow catcher (oversized bumper), you might want to dial this information in because these guys are not just trying to make a fashion statement. Also, it's important to remember that animals do not usually comes in herds of one. If you do see one, be prepared for the rest of the family.

Cartoon by Jerry King

"If I look a little pale, it's because I just sold enough blood to buy new tires for my bike."

Funnies

In addition to a few biker quips, I would like to share a few biker jokes. Frankly, jokes written down don't do much for me, other than providing material for when the situation calls for a joke. In my experience, twenty percent of a good joke is how and when the joke is delivered, in addition to whether the punch line surprises you or not. The other eighty percent is dependent on how many beers you and your buddies have had.

I will kick it off with one of my Dad's favorite jokes, which happens to be motorcycle related. My Dad loved to tell jokes, and he wasn't half bad at it. The problem was, he only knew three jokes. Needless to say, I heard them repeated often enough over the years to memorize all three! I think you'll like this one.

Dad's Joke

A trucker pulls into a mom-and-pop burger joint for a bite to eat and notices about a dozen Harleys parked out front. The bikers had had a few beers and were getting loud, so he situated himself at the other end of the bar. The largest, most tattooed one sauntered up to the trucker and started giving him crap about this and that, verbally abusing him to entertain his buddies. The trucker finished his hamburger, got up and left.

Afterward, the biker shouted to the bartender, who had a bird's eye view of the parking lot, "That trucker sure was a coward."

The bartender responded, "He can't drive worth a damn either. Just backed his rig over 10 motorcycles trying to get out of the parking lot."

Funny No. 2

A tough biker dude came upon a traffic jam

caused by a crowd of police, rescue folks, and gawkers around a high bridge. Turns out, there was a young thin lady in a short dress and loads of make-up, standing on the edge and threatening to jump to her death. The police were making no progress in talking her down. The biker pushed his way through the crowd and convinced the cops he could talk her down.

He got as close to the girl as he could and said, "Now, Sugar Shorts there is no reason for you to take your life, but if you want to, I suppose it is your decision. Could you do me one big favor first? Could you just give me one big wet kiss?"

The girl said "Sure" and gave him a big juicy kiss.

He said "Wow! That was great. Now, why would a pretty little thing like you want to take her life?"

The girl responded, "My parents are giving me a hard time about wearing girls clothes." It was unclear at this point whether the girl jumped or was pushed from the bridge.

Funny No. 3

A motorcycle patrolman was rushed to the hospital with an inflamed appendix. Doctors operated on him immediately. He came around and was relieved when they told him all had gone to plan. He was going to be fine.

After the doctor left, the patrolman felt something pulling at the hairs on his chest. He was worried that something may be wrong but he was still too weak from the surgery to do anything about it. After a few failed attempts, he managed to pull his hospital gown down enough to see what was causing the discomfort.

He looked down and saw three wide strips of ultra-adhesive tape stuck firmly to his chest. Written on the tape in large black letters was the message:

Get well soon.

*From: The nurse you gave
the ticket to last week*

P.S. – I'll be 'round to remove the tape later.

Funny No. 4

This little guy has been sitting in a bar,

staring at his drink for over an hour. Then a big, tattooed biker ambles up to the bar, takes the little guy's drink, and gulps it down. Staring down at the little guy, he says, "What are you going to do about that?"

The little guy starts to cry, and the big guy quickly softens. He says, " Oh man, I didn't mean to make you cry. I hate to see a man cry."

The little guy wipes his eyes and explains, "I woke up late this morning and missed an important meeting, so my boss fired me. When I got to the parking lot, I discovered someone had stolen my car. Well, I don't have insurance. Left my wallet in the cab that took me home; found my wife in bed with another man; and my dog bit me. I came here trying to work up enough courage to kill myself, and now you've gone and drank all my poison."

Funny No. 5

A cop was staking out a biker bar, looking for riders leaving under the influence. Near closing time, he saw a biker stumble out of the bar, trip on the curb, and fumble with his keys for 5 minutes. When he finally gets on his bike, it takes him another 5 minutes to get the key into the ignition. Meanwhile, the parking lot clears out as everyone else leaves the bar. When the fumbling biker finally pulls off, he doesn't make it more than 5 feet before the cop pulls him over. He gives the biker a Breathalyzer test and finds his blood alcohol level to be zero.

Brows furrowed, the cop looks at the biker and says, "How's this possible?"

The biker quips, "Tonight I'm the designated decoy."

Funny No. 6

Due to work, an avid rider had missed weeks of riding his bike. The weekend was upon him but to his chagrin, storms were coming in. Thinking he could beat the rain, he leathered up and fired up his Harley. When he got to the end of the drive, he turned back.

Back in the house, he took his leathers off and slipped back in bed beside his wife. He whispered, "The weather's awful out there."

She sighed, "I know, can you believe it? My stupid husband is out riding his motorcycle."

Funny No. 7

A blonde was speeding in a 35 mile-an-hour zone. The motorcycle cop that pulled her over was also a blonde. The cop asked to see her driver's license. The driver looked frantically in her purse, and eventually asked the blonde cop what they look like.

The cop said, "It has your picture on it."

The driver pulled a small mirror out of her purse, and said "Ah, this must be my driver's license."

She handed the mirror to the blonde cop, who looked at it and said, "I didn't know you were a cop." She smiled and told the driver she was free to go.

Funny No. 8

A mechanic was removing a cylinder head from the motor of a Harley when he spotted a well-known cardiologist, who was waiting for his bike to be serviced. The mechanic shouted across the garage, "Hey Doc! Come take a look at this."

The doctor walked over to where the mechanic was working, crouched by the bike. The mechanic said, "So Doc. Look at this engine. I open up its heart, take the valves out, repair any damage, and put the valves back. Then it runs like new. So how come I make $50,000 a year and you make $500,000?"

The cardiologist smiled. He leaned over and said, "Try doing all that with the engine running."

Funny No. 9

Two sisters were trying out their new high-speed crotch rocket when a cop pulled them over for going too slow. They were going exactly 21 miles per hour and had traffic backed up for miles. He asked the driver, "Why are you going so slow? You're holding up traffic."

She said, "That's the speed limit."

The cop replied, "No, blondie, this is Highway No. 21. The speed limit is 65 mph." The cop shifted his gaze to the other sister, "By the way, why is your passenger looking so pale?"

The driver replied, "Probably because we just came off Highway No. 165."

Funny No. 10

A biker finally saved up enough money to purchase the boots of his dreams. He could not wait to show them off to his wife. When he came home, he found her in the kitchen. He pranced back and forth, but he couldn't get her to notice the boots. He went to the bedroom and took off all his cloths except the boots and returned to the kitchen. She still didn't seem to notice. Frustrated, he said "don't you see anything different?"

She said, "Nope. Hanging straight down. Was yesterday and will be tomorrow."

He said, "It's looking at my new boots!"

She said, "You should've bought a helmet."

14 Reasons Why Motorcycles Are Better Than Women

1. Your motorcycles do not get upset when you forget their birthday.

2. Your motorcycle does not get upset when you ignore it for a few weeks.

3. Your motorcycle won't wake you up at 3 a.m. and ask if you love it.

4. Your motorcycle won't leave you for another rider.

5. You don't have to pay alimony to an ex-motorcycle.

6. If you say bad things to your motorcycle, you don't have to apologize before you can ride it again.

7. If your motorcycle doesn't look good, you can paint it or get better parts.

8. If your motorcycle makes too much noise, you can install a muffler.

9. If your motorcycle smokes, you can do something about it.

10. Motorcycles always feel like going for a ride.

11. Motorcycles don't care about how many motorcycles you have in the garage.

12. Motorcycles don't care if you look at other motorcycles or buy motorcycle magazines.

13. Motorcycles don't have parents.

14. When riding, you and your motorcycle both arrive at the same time.

Disclaimer

Having said all of this, I am totally confident that motorcycle women can come up with twice the reasons a motorcycle is better than a man!